Engaging the Past

TEACHING HISTORY TODAY AND IN THE FUTURE

About the Series

This series for K–12 and collegiate history teachers, educators, curriculum specialists, and preservice teacher education candidates provides information on current and future trends in the teaching and learning of history.

Books in the series explore the vast array of ideas, methods and strategies that actively engage students in learning historical content and developing skills that will help them in their education and to become competent citizens.

The volumes are aimed at professionals working or planning to work in history education at all levels of education in schools and other venues related to the teaching of history.

About the Series Editor

The **Teaching History Today and in the Future** was conceived by and is edited by Mark Newman, PhD, Professor of Studies Education, National College of Education, National Louis University, Chicago, Illinois.

Mark Newman has published articles and books on topics related to history, geography, and visual literacy. He received the 2022 Education Award from the International Visual Literacy Association and was awarded the National College of Education Distinguished Teaching Award in 2016. He has pursued his interest in history education through grants from the National Endowment for the Humanities and the Library of Congress Teaching with Primary Sources Program.

Titles in the Series

Teaching History Today: Applying the Triad of Inquiry, Primary Sources, and Literacy by Mark Newman

New Approaches in Teaching History: Using Science Fiction to Introduce Students to New Vistas in Historical Thought by Frederic Krome

Engaging the Past: Action and Interaction in the History Classroom by Elizabeth George

Engaging the Past

Action and Interaction in the History Classroom

Elizabeth George

ROWMAN & LITTLEFIELD
Lanham • Boulder • New York • London

Published by Rowman & Littlefield
An imprint of The Rowman & Littlefield Publishing Group, Inc.
4501 Forbes Boulevard, Suite 200, Lanham, Maryland 20706
www.rowman.com

86-90 Paul Street, London EC2A 4NE, United Kingdom

Copyright © 2024 by Elizabeth George

All rights reserved. No part of this book may be reproduced in any form or by any electronic or mechanical means, including information storage and retrieval systems, without written permission from the publisher, except by a reviewer who may quote passages in a review.

British Library Cataloguing in Publication Information Available

Library of Congress Cataloging-in-Publication Data

Names: George, Elizabeth, 1981– author.
Title: Engaging the past : action and interaction in the history classroom / Elizabeth George.
Other titles: Action and interaction in the history classroom
Description: Lanham : Rowman & Littlefield, [2024] | Series: Teaching history today and in the future | Includes bibliographical references. | Summary: "This book presents a variety of strategies to help teachers rethink their relationship to the content and their students. Each chapter explains an active learning approach, practical steps for how to put the approach into practice, and ideas for how teachers can customize the strategy"— Provided by publisher.
Identifiers: LCCN 2023055408 (print) | LCCN 2023055409 (ebook) | ISBN 9781475870053 (cloth) | ISBN 9781475870060 (paperback) | ISBN 9781475870077 (epub)
Subjects: LCSH: History—Study and teaching. | Active learning.
Classification: LCC D16.2 .G4375 2024 (print) | LCC D16.2 (ebook) | DDC 907.1—dc23/eng/20240110
LC record available at https://lccn.loc.gov/2023055408
LC ebook record available at https://lccn.loc.gov/2023055409

Contents

Preface	vii
Introduction	ix
Chapter 1: The You Decide Lecture	1
Chapter 2: History Lab	23
Chapter 3: Board Games for Nongamer Instructors	43
Chapter 4: Using Stories	61
Chapter 5: Visual Literacies	77
Chapter 6: Role-Playing Games and Simulations	95
Conclusion	111
About the Author	127

Preface

This is the type of book I wish someone had handed me when I was starting my teaching career. I was passionate about history but had mostly been taught through lecture-based classes. I stuck with it because I loved the subject, but I could see why many people thought of history as interminably dull.

Although I heard a handful of truly brilliant lectures in college, the learning that stuck with me the most was related to work that I did, either alone or with a group. During my first few years of teaching, I was dismayed to see students falling asleep and checking out as I worked hard at lecturing. How could something I loved so much be coming across as so boring?

Over the course of many years, workshops, conversations, books, articles, and conferences, I developed a learner-centered pedagogy—one where I feel my students and I are on the same wavelength regarding the excitement and intrigue of history. However, it took far too long, and I bored far too many students before developing the mindset outlined in this book. It was all the more frustrating because the scholarly discussion about learner-centered history pedagogy is decades old, yet it still took me several years of teaching to discover it. *Engaging the Past* is an attempt to contribute to, synthesize, and popularize teaching strategies for instructors who want to create active and interactive classrooms where students engage deeply with history.

In this book I purposely present only six specific strategies. There are many books and resources that present dozens or more. For beginning teachers, however, there is value to looking at a more limited menu of approaches, developing them well, and being able to rotate through them frequently. Having just a few tried and true strategies limits prep time and allows students to practice the intended skills several times throughout the course. All of the strategies in the following chapters can be further customized to provide variety or spark thinking about new approaches altogether.

This book is the result of many conversations with colleagues at MidAmerica Nazarene University and Taylor University. I am grateful to Mark Hamilton at MidAmerica who started me on this path, as well as the support of Barb Bird and the Bedi Center for Teaching and Learning Excellence at Taylor. Other friends and colleagues read sections and gave feedback, including Mark Hayse, Ben Wetzel, Jakob Miller, Katie Husby, and Melissa Stroud, along with the series editor Mark Newman. Sarah Bushey's careful editing eye was impressive even back when she was one of my students, and she made every page of this book better. At Rowman & Littlefield, Tom Koerner, April Snider, and Jasmine Holman supported the project and guided its completion.

Many students, perhaps unwittingly, gave me feedback on the ideas in this book. Friends and family supported me along the way, especially my husband, Ryan George, who has always been an unfailing champion of my career. My kids, Juliana and RJ, inspire me to be a better teacher and make sure the world is full of great teachers.

Introduction

The belief that history is a dull subject is so pervasive that it has become a familiar stereotype, with famous examples ranging from the history teacher in *Ferris Bueller's Day Off* to Professor Binns in Harry Potter. Despite the stereotype, many adults would agree that history is important and wish they had paid better attention in school. To reach students and increase interest in history as the valuable and relevant discipline that it is, instructors must bring students into the *doing* of history. While young people may experience history informally at museums and historic sites, the center of history education is the classroom. Therefore, it is imperative that teachers are intentional and informed about how they teach history.

Many instructors feel hesitant about incorporating methods that they are unfamiliar with or that rely on student energy and participation in order to work. Most teachers feel confident in reading lecture notes and showing slide presentations. Students know they are supposed to be quiet and perhaps write things down. The instructor feels in control of both the classroom and the content that is "covered."[1] Instructors may therefore be reluctant to add projects and activities that require additional skills from both students and teachers. Additionally, they might not feel like an expert and may worry about seeming less authoritative in front of the class.

On the other side of that fear, however, is the opportunity to awaken students to the excitement of real history—of using historical research skills to answer real questions and developing historical thinking in order to understand the world more deeply. Instructors do not need to be experts in everything. They can choose a few areas in which to develop their skills, have the humility to recognize that everything might not be amazing the first time, and position themselves as co-learners with their students. The result is a whole new subject of exploration for students and deeper fulfillment in work for the teacher—in short, real engagement with the discipline of history.

Engaging the Past's pedagogical contribution is not an attempt to argue whether students receive good grades and learn facts effectively in lecture-based classes. Many students are adept at navigating a lecture class and getting satisfactory grades. Plenty of students would prefer to not have their rhythms disrupted when they feel they have mastered how to learn a subject.[2] Rather, this book is an invitation to instructors to spark interest in history, show students the many facets of history, and encourage students to make their own contributions to the discipline. In the interest of preserving and expanding the historical profession, instructors must broaden its appeal or find more ways to welcome new young scholars.

This is a book about teaching historical thinking. The motivation is not active learning just for the sake of having a lively classroom. Rather, the inspiration derives from a commitment to transforming how students think about history. There are many ways to define and describe the components of historical thinking. A simple way to think about it is the difference between what a trained historian sees when they encounter a new historical document or artifact and what a novice historian sees. The trained historian can understand and contemplate the item on many levels, generating questions and connections. While those highly honed skills are the result of years of work, study, and practice, the basic components and skills are available to novice and beginning historians as well. The instructor simply needs to teach students the skills, which is best done by showing, not telling.

Many teachers and professors work hard to teach their students how to think historically. Balancing content coverage and skills is one of the central challenges for history teachers. Many teachers at least attempt to convey and give their students opportunities to practice the "five Cs of historical thinking," that is "change over time, causality, context, complexity, and contingency."[3] The idea is to help students become cognizant of these factors when thinking about historical events, ideas, people, and evidence. These skills help students develop the ability to read historical documents more deeply, make better arguments, and apply more accurate historical understanding to present problems.

Sam Wineburg is one of the leading scholars helping instructors understand how to teach historical thinking. For Wineburg, the issue is particularly critical, and historical thinking is not simply an updated way to teach history. He argues that "history offers a storehouse of complex and rich problems, not unlike those that confront us daily in the social world. Examining these problems requires an interpretive acumen that extends beyond the 'locate information in the text' skills that dominate many school tasks."[4]

For Wineburg, the practical work of historical thinking involves approaching historical documents by using the following strategies: "sourcing, contextualizing, close reading, using background knowledge, reading the silences, and corroborating."[5] Practicing these methods allows students to participate in the work that historians do, even at a beginner level. Historical thinking pushes back against the idea that students must accrue a massive foundation of memorized facts before they can "do history."

Historical thinking is more than just a snazzy veneer on traditional history teaching. The approach incentivizes both learning and teaching on several levels. One important way this happens is by helping students exchange the foundational idea that history was an inevitable unfolding of events with the much more accurate understanding that historians construct history.

Students must learn (1) that history is constructed, (2) how history is constructed, (3) how they too can construct history. Nevertheless, traditional history instruction seems to stubbornly cling to the idea that students need a massive foundation of factual knowledge before they can do history. To achieve this, teachers tell students uncontested history narratives for years before showing them that historians use specific skills to construct history and the resulting narratives are subject to debate. Beyond some document-based essay assignments or simple research papers, students are rarely invited to try their hand at constructing history.

It is no wonder, then, that it is difficult to disabuse students of the notion that history is just a boring parade of facts. While of course there needs to be a balance between historical literacy (i.e., knowledge of names, dates, events, and ideas) and discovery so that students do not constantly reinvent the wheel, nevertheless, an active and interactive classroom that draws students into the action of doing history is better for students, teachers, and the longevity of the discipline.[6]

Why create classrooms focused on action and interaction? Why not simply include more historiography in lectures? There are several motivations to provide active and interactive learning experiences. One motive has become a bit of a mantra among active learning advocates: "the one who does the work does the learning."[7] This is not to say that doing random busywork assignments results in learning or that listening can never result in learning. It means, rather, that instructors must create intentional, motivating learning experiences in which students are working as much as, if not more than, the instructor.

This principle is intuitive for most aspects of learning. To learn to swim, there is a limit to how much you can talk about it; at some point you have to get in the pool. To read, there is only so much that someone can read to you; eventually you need to try to decode the words. The only way to learn to walk is to stop being carried around. Humans live the effectiveness of this principle, and it is just as true when it comes to understanding what history really is. At some point, you have to do it.

Nevertheless, when it comes to a real classroom, it is easy for instructors to feel that students are actively engaged, even without requiring much evidence of their engagement. The instructor may be working very hard in lecturing and feel very engaged herself, and it is difficult to imagine that all the people in the room do not feel the same way.

By contrast, the active learning approach encourages instructors to take on several different roles in the classroom, often within the same class session. In many cases, the instructor needs to take on the role of expert, particularly to teach and reinforce concepts and skills related to historical thinking. While teachers can cultivate a classroom that relies on student energy and creativity, it is still the instructor's job to hold the line on historical accuracy, reinforce the importance of understanding historical context, and decide which historical thinking strategies are most relevant to the task at hand.

There are also instances, however, when it is better for the instructor to act as co-learner. This position may be difficult for teachers to assume, since it may feel like a loss of control and authority, especially at first. Nevertheless, when instructors act as co-learners—asking questions, exploring partially developed ideas, admitting a lack of knowledge—they demystify the historical thinking process for students. As a co-learner, the instructor will still use their skills as a historian, but they do it in a way that is, as Wineburg explains, "making thinking visible."[8] In so doing, they communicate to students that the classroom community is figuring out answers together.

The goal in acting as a co-learner is not to do the thinking for students but instead to think alongside students, guiding them along the path to historical discovery. When students get to see repeated demonstrations of historical thinking in action, they will have a much better sense of how to develop the skill themselves. Since most students are exposed to history as an already-settled narrative, they do not naturally realize that the process of discovery and reinterpretation is open to all who do history.

Another motive for building an active and interactive classroom is to counteract students' tendencies to become adept at paying "civil attention." Jay Howard notes that "civil attention" represents the unspoken agreement between students and instructor that "so long as students appear to be listening, they can expect that the professor won't call on them unless they signal a willingness to participate."[9] In a classroom where civil attention becomes the norm, Howard notes, only about five to eight students provide most of the active participation, regardless of class size. Still, that small number is enough that an instructor might feel that the class was learning, even if assessment would reveal that most were not.

It benefits the instructor to work with students' rhythms of attention. James Lang presents the intriguing idea that teachers should think of attention as a commodity to be spent or saved in the classroom. Instructors can structure their lessons to cultivate, steer, and refresh student attention so that class time is used efficiently and effectively. Being attuned to students' attention rhythms also creates a more equitable classroom, Lang notes, as it does not punish students whose attention naturally starts to wane. Working with, rather than against, students' rhythms is also more fulfilling for teachers. The feeling of having the whole class engaged is much more life- and career-affirming than feeling as if no one cares what you are doing.[10]

An active and interactive classroom is also driven by care for students. Students who feel the instructor cares about their learning and have opportunities to make personal connections with the instructor and fellow students will feel more comfortable about taking the risks needed to do deep learning.[11] While every teacher has their own ways to demonstrate care for students, there are several strategies that most effective teachers use. Knowing and using students' names is obvious but can be difficult when the number of students is in the hundreds each semester. Telling students that knowing their names is a priority and asking them to help the instructor learn names can help build the initial connection.

In a similar vein, knowing students' interests and worldviews and incorporating them into class discussions helps to build a connection. It is important for the instructor to not assume they understand their students just because they teach them. Rather, talking with students and creating opportunities for them to discuss ideas and interests with each other helps create a learning environment that is relevant and welcoming.

Other strategies that help to foster a safe and effective learning space include having a great first day and being organized in all aspects of the course.[12] Both can be difficult for instructors who are not naturally extroverted or organized. However, having the ultimate goal in mind of an active and interactive classroom where students practice higher order thinking skills can motivate the instructor to remove unnecessary obstacles and help students feel comfortable and ready to learn right away.

Many students appreciate having a variety of learning activities and opportunities that allow different students to shine and all students to make a meaningful connection to the material. Offering various ways to learn and demonstrate learning helps reduce anxiety as students realize that doing poorly on one type of assignment does not mean that they should give up; they might learn better from a different type of assignment. Informing students early on that they will experience many different learning opportunities also helps them calibrate their expectations for the course.

Finally, teachers should use technology as a tool, not as a crutch or substitute for real lessons. While the options for technology-optimized lessons are endless and often freely available, using technology excessively can make it more difficult for instructors to demonstrate care for students. Striking a balance between everyone looking at a screen and everyone looking at each other or engaging in a more tactile experience (even writing on paper!) can help set the classroom experience apart as something special and worth students' time and attention.

As much as students need care to be active and interactive in their learning, teachers also need care in order to prevent burnout and to have the resources to teach their students well. Some learning strategies are so time-consuming and labor-intensive that they are not feasible for teachers who are already busy. In addition, many teachers might avoid active learning because it seems like the grading would be overwhelming. There are two ways in which the strategies outlined in this book consider the flourishing of teachers as well as students.

First, for many teachers, experiencing students who are paying attention, learning, and being transformed motivates them to seek out more effective ways to teach. The feeling of succeeding as a teacher, instead of just completing tasks or covering material, is life-giving and energizing. For many teachers, the energy and well-being that comes from succeeding in their career is worth the risk of changing strategies and trying to improve.

Second, teachers should recognize and seek to limit the burden of grading.[13] There are many ways for students to complete a learning experience successfully without the instructor needing to spend hours grading artifacts that represent that success. Instructors should carefully consider whether students will use instructor feedback to improve or if the learning was centered on completing the activity or assignment. In those kinds of cases, instructors can use complete / incomplete grades or rely heavily on rubrics to assign grades.

For other assignments, the instructor should think of grading time much in the same way as student attention—a commodity to be spent or saved. If it is worthwhile for the instructor to spend hours giving extensive feedback, then the instructor should also close the learning loop with students so that they learn from the feedback.

Many of the activities outlined in this book include both formative and summative assessments.[14] The instructor should spend minimal time grading assessments for which the purpose is to give students opportunities to practice a skill, rather than demonstrate mastery. Instead of marking every submission, instructors can reserve feedback for class time, particularly if a significant portion of the class missed the goal. While summative assessments will need full grading attention, it is also true that creative assignments are often—though not always—more fun and interesting to grade. Considering carefully how much grades and feedback will lead to an increase in student learning should help instructors be intentional about how much and what they grade.

This book provides several practical strategies for embracing historical thinking as the foundation of history classes. It is best used in concert with other course design strategies, such as backward course design and universal design for learning (UDL), that help teachers design effective learning goals. The chapters that follow outline active and interactive ways to help students achieve a variety of course objectives related to historical thinking.

Chapter 1 presents the You Decide lecture, an interactive strategy for teaching historical thinking skills steeped in historical literacy. In this approach, students are immersed in historical events and take on the perspectives of various historical actors. The instructor leads students through selected decision moments in which the students are set up to recognize how historical actors' choices were constrained by various contingencies. The strategy aims to keep all students attentive to the course content while also giving them opportunities to do history through analyzing documents and recognizing the validity of contrasting perspectives.

Chapter 2 offers instructions and practices to implement regular history labs into history classes. History labs allow students to investigate historical events more deeply by analyzing sets of documents that are as lightly curated as possible. This attempt to mimic real archival research guides students through the process of reading documents in the context of the larger source set and allowing their findings to shape their arguments. Students are encouraged to allow the evidence to shape the conclusions, not cherry-pick quotes to fit into predetermined arguments.

Chapter 3 shows how even instructors who are not "gamers" can use board games in the classroom. Board games present an intriguing and accessible way for students to consider how history is presented for popular consumption. Many sophisticated board games about a variety of historical topics exist, but instructors who do not regularly play board games personally may be hesitant to use them in the classroom. The chapter shows how instructors can use board games to achieve learning goals related to both content mastery and historical thinking skills and how nongamers can find creative ways to harness the benefits of board games.

Chapter 4 encourages instructors to use exciting and absorbing stories not simply as examples but as the underlying structure of a whole lesson or even a unit. It shows how the deliberate use of stories can help students understand how historians construct history and how historians contest narratives. With this strategy, students participate in the process of creating narratives and are exposed to the importance of context and perspective in interpreting the past. By doing history under the instructor's guidance, students have the freedom to question accepted narratives and ponder how historians might interpret events in different ways.

Chapter 5 discusses the importance of developing visual literacy, even for novice historians. Images provide many benefits to history instruction due to their accessibility and attention-grabbing nature; however, teachers should not assume that students can "read" images without training. Spending time teaching visual literacy allows instructors to act as co-learners with students, use images to develop students' historical thinking, and incorporate a variety of visual sources into history courses. By equipping students with visual literacy skills, instructors prepare students to interrogate an increasingly visual world as well as recognize how images provide a unique window into the past.

Chapter 6 explores the benefits of the Reacting to the Past role-playing pedagogy and how a Reacting mindset can shape course activities and assignments, even if the instructor does not use any role-playing games in the classroom. The chapter discusses the potency of this high-impact practice and the instructor's critical role in helping students succeed and reap maximum learning benefits. The chapter also shows that the same work that sets students up for success in Reacting games can transform lackluster class activities into powerful and engaging interactive learning experiences.

Each chapter includes an "In Theory" section to enter into the conversations scholars are already having about these ideas and strategies. The "In Practice" section explains the approach and the connections to historical skills and includes examples. "Customize" presents ideas for teachers to make each strategy their own, with further ideas for adaptations or variations. The goal of the book is to help instructors feel equipped to create engaging classrooms that emphasize the practice of history and the importance of historical thinking.

NOTES

1. Lendol Calder, "Uncoverage: Toward a Signature Pedagogy for the History Survey," *The Journal of American History* 92, no. 4 (March 2006): 1358–70, https://doi.org/10.2307/4485896. In 2006 Calder wrote, "It is a good moment to remind ourselves what the introductory survey could be (and what it already is for some teachers) if we replaced generic pedagogies of coverage with teaching and learning marked by the distinctive signature of history" (1360). See also Joel M. Sipress and David J. Voelker, "The End of the History Survey Course: The Rise and Fall of the Coverage Model," *The Journal of American History* 97, no. 4 (2011): 1050–66, https://www.jstor.org/stable/41508915.

2. Louis Deslauriers, Logan S. McCarty, Kelly Miller, Kristina Callaghan, and Greg Kestin, "Measuring Actual Learning versus Feeling of Learning in Response to Being Actively Engaged in the Classroom," *Proceedings of the National Academy of Sciences* 116, no. 39 (September 2019): 19251–57.

3. Thomas Andrews and Flannery Burke, "What Does It Mean to Think Historically?," *Perspectives on History*, January 1, 2007, https://www.historians.org/publications-and-directories/perspectives-on-history/january-2007/what-does-it-mean-to-think-historically.

4. Sam Wineburg, *Historical Thinking and Other Unnatural Acts: Charting the Future of Teaching the Past* (Philadelphia: Temple University Press, 2001), 51.

5. Sam Wineburg, "Thinking Like a Historian," *Teaching with Primary Sources Quarterly* 3, no. 1 (Winter 2010): 3.

6. Jennifer Wiley and Ivan K. Ash, "Multimedia Learning of History," in *The Cambridge Handbook of Multimedia Learning*, ed. Richard E. Mayer (Cambridge: Cambridge University Press, 2005): 376, https://doi.org/10.1017/CBO9780511816819.025.

7. Terry Doyle, *Learner-Centered Teaching: Putting the Research on Learning into Practice* (New York: Routledge, 2011), 3.

8. Wineburg, "Thinking Like a Historian," 3.

9. Jay Howard, "How to Hold a Better Class Discussion," *The Chronicle of Higher Education*, May 23, 2019, https://www.chronicle.com/article/how-to-hold-a-better-class-discussion/.

10. James M. Lang, *Distracted: Why Students Can't Focus and What You Can Do about It* (New York: Hachette Book Group, 2020), 149, 153, 179.

11. Steven A. Meyers, "Do Your Students Care Whether You Care about Them?," *College Teaching* 57, no. 4 (Fall 2009): 205–10; Amy Chasteen Miller and Brooklyn Mills, "'If They Don't Care, I Don't Care': Millennial and Generation Z Students and the Impact of Faculty Caring," *Journal of the Scholarship of Teaching and Learning* 19, no. 4 (October 2019): 78–89; Ashley Grantham, Emily Erin Robinson, and Diane Chapman, "'That Truly Meant a Lot to Me': A Qualitative Examination of Meaningful Faculty-Student Interactions," *College Teaching* 63, no. 3 (July 2015): 125–32.

12. James M. Lang, "How to Teach a Good First Day of Class," *The Chronicle of Higher Education*, accessed July 22, 2023, https://www.chronicle.com/article/how-to-teach-a-good-first-day-of-class/.

13. John Jerrim and Sam Sims, "When Is High Workload Bad for Teacher Wellbeing? Accounting for the Non-Linear Contribution of Specific Teaching Tasks," *Teaching & Teacher Education* 105 (September 2021), https://doi.org/10.1016/j.tate.2021.103395.

14. Dante D. Dixson and Frank C. Worrell, "Formative and Summative Assessment in the Classroom," *Theory Into Practice* 55, no. 2 (Spring 2016): 153–59.

Chapter 1

The You Decide Lecture

The year is 1968. In a suburban American living room, a father stares down his teenaged son as the mother perches nervously on the couch. Strains of Jimi Hendrix's "All Along the Watchtower" float down the hall from one of the bedrooms. The father breaks his silence to vent his frustration at his son: "First those protests at college and now you bring that music into the house to 'enlighten' your sister. Tell me exactly what we are paying for!" He paces in front of his son, then stops to issue a warning in a voice that is almost too calm: "That's two."

This exchange—though one might be able to picture it within the historical context of the United States in 1968—actually occurred in a college classroom in 2021. The parents and son in the scenario were college students. They were not acting in a play or reading a story; rather, their exchange was both spontaneous and orchestrated as part of a teaching approach called the You Decide lecture.

This chapter explores what a You Decide lecture is, the research and pedagogical choices behind the approach, how to put it into practice, and how instructors can adapt the methodology to make it their own.

IN THEORY

This strategy is designed to show students that history is choices. It places students within real historical situations and challenges them to take on the characteristics of historical actors and make choices based on real events. By experiencing the complexities of decision-making, students realize on both an emotional and intellectual level that the course of historical events is not inevitable; instead, history consists of a series of choices made by real people. This realization leads students to recognize that they are now part of choices that will shape future narratives of the past.

The teaching strategy derives from two ideas: the Choose Your Own Adventure books that were especially popular in the 1980s and a pedagogical approach called "Creating Lives," as outlined by historian Edith Sheffer.

In Choose Your Own Adventure books, the reader is the main character in the story, and every few pages they are faced with a choice, such as one from *Journey Under the Sea* (1978), in which the reader is given the character of an Atlantis-seeking deep-sea diver. The diver explores for a couple of paragraphs and then is faced with this choice on page 2:

> If you decide to explore the ledge where the Seeker has come to rest, turn to page 6.
> If you decide to cut loose from the Maray and dive with the Seeker into the canyon in the ocean floor, turn to page 4.[1]

The reader makes their choice, and the adventure continues. While certainly entertaining to a generation of pre-internet readers, the books were highly structured to keep the adventure going. All Choose Your Own Adventure books function based on a decision tree, where choices bring the reader along various paths, opening up some options and closing down others.[2]

In a similar vein, Edith Sheffer's "Creating Lives" approach to structuring college history courses begins with students creating historical avatars. They keep those avatars throughout the whole term and experience the course subject through the eyes of their avatar. In her articles outlining the approach, Sheffer offers examples from her course titled "Germany & The World Wars" where students create avatars of German citizens and experience the events of the wars through readings and lectures and then respond to readings and events in their avatar's diary entries.[3]

The You Decide lecture uses the idea of characters that make choices but offers the flexibility of changing the characters and the historical context for each class period. It combines the excitement of the Choose Your Own Adventure books with strict historical accuracy.

Practicing the skills of making connections, incorporating historical context, and recognizing the agency of historical actors makes history more exciting to learn and more applicable to the present. A You Decide lecture brings those historical analysis skills together by giving students the opportunity to apply them in real-world, historically accurate scenarios. The You Decide format relates to all five Cs of historical thinking, but most directly to contingency or the "claim that every historical outcome depends upon a number of prior conditions; that each of these prior conditions depends, in turn, upon still other conditions; and so on."[4]

The importance of individual choice is a significant aspect of contingency. You Decide lectures emphasize the importance of individual choices as well as how contingent they are on other events and choices. By establishing students as historically plausible characters in the real historical record, students see how—even if they personally want to make a different choice—they are constrained by the historical contingencies of their character, the time period, and the events.

One of the difficulties with teaching history is fighting against hindsight bias in two particular ways. First, the phenomenon known as "creeping determinism" or "necessity impressions" is the sense humans have, in hindsight, that an event was inevitable. Similarly, social psychologists point out the potency of "foreseeability impressions" or the "I-knew-it-all-along effect," where it is hard to imagine any other outcome once the outcome is known.[5] We can see both of these psychological phenomena at work in how some students perceive history and even in how some teachers teach it.

One example relates to how students think about the Japanese bombing of Pearl Harbor. In December 1941, many Americans perceived the event as terrifying, anxiety-inducing, and psychologically overwhelming. When students learn about it now, however, it is easy to slip into the perception that Japan made a laughably off-the-mark miscalculation in challenging a future global superpower. The U.S. defeat of Japan seems so inevitable that Pearl Harbor seems merely an exciting opening scene in a story where the right side wins.

Because of hindsight bias, it is easy for instructors to present history as a clear set of "right" and "wrong" decisions, even if the people at the time did not know how their decisions would turn out. That presentation of history, however, does nothing to help students see the individual's role or the difficulty in making choices when the end of the story is unknown; it seems like it does not matter what individuals chose to do because the outcome was inevitable. It also makes history seem more like a fairy tale of good versus evil, rather than a complex, interconnected, contingent web of decisions and events.[6]

The You Decide lecture format helps to emphasize the seemingly simple idea that history is choices. While the idea seems straightforward, due to hindsight bias and the persistent idea that history is a flat narrative of names and dates, the role of choice or "contingency" is one of the more difficult historical thinking skills to teach. Despite the difficulties, this idea of contingency is particularly relevant to students' lives because, as Thomas Andrews and Flannery Burke note, it impresses upon students the idea that "the future is up for grabs."[7]

By reinforcing that each historical event was a result of individual and collective decisions, students are dissuaded from the idea of inevitability and start to see themselves as playing a role in the human story. Bringing this relevance into the history classroom infuses lessons with urgency and anticipation, rather than boredom and repetition.

Emphasizing the role of individual choices in teaching history is not a new idea. Since the 1970s, the organization Facing History and Ourselves provides resources for teachers to explore the idea that "People Make Choices. Choices Make History."[8] Facing History and Ourselves focuses in particular on issues connected to racism and bigotry in historical events.

Similarly, the Choices Program, affiliated with the History Department at Brown University, seeks to provide curricula that emphasize the roles of multiple perspectives and stakeholders in historical events. One of the stated goals of the program is that students will "realize that all individuals are decision makers, but that personal and public choices are often restricted by time, place and circumstance."[9]

These programs and others like them provide valuable resources and packaged materials that help instructors teach contingency.[10] The You Decide lecture is not in competition with these approaches; rather, it is a format that can be adapted to many different topics and used in a variety of ways to infuse contingency into many types of history lessons.

IN PRACTICE

The section above outlined the scholarly work that provides the backdrop for the approach, but how does it actually work in the classroom? This section includes explanations for how to put the You Decide lecture into practice, including examples for each step.

In brief, the You Decide lecture has roles for everyone in the classroom learning community. The teacher sets the scenario, provides some degree of guidance for the characters, sets the decision moments, and is vigilant about maintaining historical accuracy. The students decide which characters to take within the proscribed limits, respond to the choices, discuss with their peers, and explain their choices either verbally, in writing, or both. When the format is working well, students and teacher are all working equally to make the class session successful.

Setting Scenarios

The possibilities for You Decide scenarios are almost endless. The most important principle is to discuss an event or series of events where people made choices—that is, individuals had to choose between two or more viable options. If the options are contingent from one choice to the next, all the better. It is easiest to start with scenarios that cover a relatively short period of time because as the years pass, the characters who are making choices need to either grow older or they need to change into different characters.

This chapter's opening vignette provides an example of a scenario about a relatively short time period. The scenario that resulted in the teenager facing off against his parents was part of a lesson designed to teach, in particular, the concept of the "generation gap" that developed between parents and children in the 1960s and, more generally, the turbulence of the 1960s in the United States.

The lesson opens with students choosing characters: in this case, two parents and a teenager (more on creating characters below). The lesson begins with television news footage about John F. Kennedy's assassination. The instructor discusses Lyndon Johnson's early presidency, and then the parents in the group are asked who they will vote for in 1964 (more on setting choices below). This first choice starts to determine how the "parents" will respond to the subsequent events. The instructor brings the class through key events leading to 1968 and reminds the class that the "teenager" is now eighteen years old.

The next choice purposefully pits the parents against the teenager as the class is told that the teen participated in an antiwar protest while at college, and the family needs to respond. In this situation, many "fathers" reprimand the "teenager" with something along the lines of "Why are we paying all this money for you to goof around at college?" With the family now at odds, the teacher introduces the topic of music in the 1960s and plays a few popular songs. That information sets up the You Decide choice that created the opening scene:

> **You Decide!** Parents: you hear these songs streaming from the radio in your youngest child's room. They tell you that the teenager introduced them to this music. How do you respond?

Students seem to particularly enjoy berating their "teenager" about their music choices, and the "teens" get defensive and respond that the parents do not understand. In one memorable interaction, dramatized in the opening to this chapter, the student playing the father stared down the teenager, held up two fingers, and said coldly, "That's two"—meaning one more strike and the teenager would be kicked out of the house. There was a very tense pause before the group devolved into laughter.

This lived experience sets up the perfect moment for the instructor to introduce the phrase "generation gap" and explain where it factored more or less potently throughout the twentieth century. Because students felt the disconnect between the parents and the teenager develop over the course of the lesson, they are more likely to remember the concept and use it correctly themselves.

There are, of course, many ways to find scenarios. Consider instances in history where one person or group needed support from another, such as when explorers needed support from monarchs or when women tried to change laws that affected their status. Alternatively, consider instances where two or more groups disagreed. For example, almost any instance where a leader is trying to rally support for a war, or when minority groups were trying to determine the most effective ways to protest can work for a You Decide lecture.

It is fairly straightforward to adapt an existing narrative-heavy lecture into the You Decide format. The instructor should choose a few decision points to focus on and work from there to create the characters and the decision options. Most of all, teachers should think about the points of the lesson that need the most emphasis to achieve learning goals (such as the generation gap in the example above) and make the choices culminate at that moment. Those high points can occur more than once in the lesson.

For example, in the scenario above about the 1960s, the lesson continued with an explanation of women's roles. The mothers in the group had to wrestle with their stance on second-wave feminism, particularly in light of the choices they made earlier in the lesson about politics and Vietnam. Some "couples" find themselves so at odds that they announce to the class that they are divorcing, which gives the instructor an opportunity to discuss the higher-than-previous divorce rates of the 1970s.

In setting the scenarios, the instructor must be vigilant about keeping the details and situations historically accurate. As the class discusses various options and responses, instructors have an important opportunity to provide guidance when answers or ideas are ahistorical.

Keeping the scenarios historically accurate might mean using video or audio clips (if available) to immerse students in the history or using pictures or artwork to represent the time period. For students without a lot of historical knowledge, limiting options is perhaps the easiest way to ensure historical accuracy. For students with more content knowledge, having a wider range of choices gives them more options to weigh and discuss.[11]

Creating Characters

Once instructors choose topics and key ideas that would work well in the You Decide format, the next step is to create characters who will navigate the scenarios and make decisions. There are several ways to go about creating characters, and additional customization will doubtless reveal more methods as well. The options provided here can be followed exactly or used as a starting point to develop other strategies.

The goal in creating characters is to give students a historically accurate figure to identify with and be emotionally connected to throughout the lesson. Rather than experiencing historical events objectively, their experience will be subject to their character's attributes. Students will also be able to compare their experience to other types of characters, as personified by their classmates.[12] For example, in the generation gap scenario explained above, the father and the teenager experienced and responded to the turbulence of the 1960s very differently.

The goal of using characters is to show the importance of perspective in how historical actors lived through and remembered events. When there are several characters discussing events in the same group, students can easily see how and why one person ends up interpreting events quite differently from another. Understanding the legitimacy of another person's perspective is one of the key skills that students gain by studying history.[13]

There are several basic options for creating characters.

Option 1

The instructor develops the characters and students only choose which character they want to be. Follow these instructions to begin the generation gap lesson discussed above.

You Decide! Family Identity:

- Your group is a family: parents and teenager
- Decide on your ethnicity and home state. (Remember: interracial marriage is illegal in some states. States that never had laws banning interracial marriage include Connecticut, New Hampshire, New York, New Jersey, Vermont, Wisconsin, Minnesota.)

Family Member Characteristics:

- *Dad*: You were born in 1924. You were five years old when the stock market crashed, and you were twenty-one in 1945. You fought in World War II in the Pacific and married a girl from your hometown as soon as the war ended. In 1963 you are thirty-nine. You work for the postal service. You voted for Truman in 1948 and Eisenhower in 1952.
- *Mom*: You were born in 1926. You were three years old when the stock market crashed. You were twenty when you got married in 1946. You had your first child at the end of 1946, and you had two more children in 1948 and 1950. In 1963, you are thirty-seven and work as a stay-at-home mom. You do a lot of volunteer work outside the home. You voted for Truman in 1948 and Eisenhower in 1952.
- *Son or Daughter*: You were born in 1946. You are the oldest child and have two younger siblings. You are seventeen in 1963. The United States has

been involved in the Cold War for your whole life, and you have grown up hearing vague information about Vietnam. You work a little in the summers babysitting or mowing lawns to earn spending money.

In this option, the characters are all set, with no customization or input from students. Because of the lesson's learning goals, the character information focuses on economics and politics and hints at the different childhoods of the parents and the teenager. The characters are designed to respond to the events of the 1960s differently, and because they are a family, they have reasons to discuss their differences.[14] Since the lesson progresses from 1964 to 1968, it is important to provide milestone years and ages.

Setting up the characters can also be a way to review the history leading up to the 1960s. Before launching into the scenario, instructors can ask the class about events such as the Korean War and the baby boom so that students can orient themselves within their roles. Instructors can also discuss how ethnicity and location might change how characters experience specific events.

There are pros and cons to the instructor providing most of the character information. On the pro side, the instructor can make sure that the characters are historically accurate and that the aspects of the characters that are most relevant (in this scenario: economics and politics) are clearly established. On the con side, since students do not have much input into their characters, they might feel less emotionally connected to the character, and they do not have the opportunity to see how choices made earlier in life affect the range of options available later in life.

For example, if the student playing the father could choose his occupation, that might change how he responds to the teenager "wasting" his money at college. Or if the mother character was able to choose a more progressive career path, she might advocate more forcefully for women's rights when that scenario is presented.

Option 2

The instructor gives students a range of choices in creating their characters. Often, lower-level students do not have enough historical knowledge to create a historically accurate character for any given scenario from scratch. Presenting a range of historically accurate choices gives students the benefits of choosing but without the danger of creating historically inaccurate characters. A range of choices also guides students to make decisions about criteria that are most relevant to the lesson. By way of example, consider the instructions for creating characters in a lesson on the United States and World War I:

You Decide! Your group is a family. Discuss and write down your answers to the following questions:

1. Choose: You are parents and a teenager *OR* You are a married couple with an older live-in parent.
2. Choose your ethnicity, and decide if you are recent immigrants.
3. Determine your economic status. Left side of the room: wealthy business owners; middle of the room: the husband is a teacher, and the wife doesn't work; right side of the room: everyone works in a factory.
4. Did the members of your family vote for Woodrow Wilson in 1912?
5. How would each member of your family feel about the United States joining a war in Europe? Why?

This option provides students with a range of choices while also ensuring that they think about politics, economics, ethnicity, gender, and class. Often, when students have the option to choose their economic status, they either choose "comfortably middle class" or "dominantly rich," so it is more effective to create a range within the classroom if the learning goals relate to economics. Establishing differences also elicits debate across the economic groups.

For example, later in the same lesson, the instructor might lead students through an analysis of World War I propaganda posters. The posters' admonitions to work hard in order to win the war will strike the factory workers differently from how the wealthy business owners will receive the message. Providing a range of choices at the beginning also helps students to see how a chain of choices can lead to different outcomes. At the end of the lesson when students have to decide their opinion about the United States joining the League of Nations, the degree of progressivism in earlier choices eithers widens or narrows their range of responses.

Providing a range of choices in creating characters has pros and cons. On the negative side, it can take longer to set up the lesson if groups need to discuss and decide on a range of options. In addition, if the options give students too much latitude, there is a greater likelihood that they will create a character that is ahistorical, particularly if students do not have strong knowledge of the time period.

On the positive side, the more that students create their own character, the more invested in the character they become. This is an important positive to consider, because creating an emotional connection between the student and the history is at the heart of the You Decide lecture; therefore, instructors should consider any strategy to foster that connection.[15] This might include giving the character a historically plausible name, as in this example from a lesson on the U.S. Market Revolution in the early nineteenth century. The instructions show a range of choices and a few ways to emotionally connect—by naming the character and introducing themselves in first person to others.

You Decide! It is 1820. You are white, eighteen years old, and you live on a farm in the Northeast with your parents and siblings.

1. Are you male or female?
2. Which of the following describes your family's (parents' and siblings') economic condition?
   a. We are poor but we manage.
   b. We've been pretty successful over the past few years.
   c. We are poor and looking for new opportunities.
   d. We've had some challenges, and it's up to me to take care of my family.
3. What is your name?

Common names in 1820: Mary, Elizabeth, Sarah, Martha, Margaret, Nancy, Catherine, Ann, Jane, Susan, and John, William, James, George, Charles, Thomas, Henry, Joseph, Samuel, David

4. Introduce yourself in character to someone nearby.

In this example, students make some choices about gender and economic status, but the choices are still constrained to keep them historically accurate.

Option 3

Rather than having students keep their character for the whole lesson, the character changes for each decision. With this option, everyone experiences the lesson from multiple points of view. This can also be a good choice to show two sides of a debate or to consider the point of view of someone who holds an unpopular opinion.

To use this option, the instructor provides the character information for each choice, and, particularly in the interests of efficient time management, students do not make any decisions about their characters. By way of example, what follows are four successive choices in a lesson about Andrew Carnegie and the Homestead strike. The lesson starts by discussing Carnegie's rise from a poor childhood to fantastic wealth. Students then see the following prompt:

You Decide! You are a poor twelve-year-old in 1880, and you know of Andrew Carnegie's fantastic success. Do you think your life could follow a similar path? Why or why not?

The point is to evaluate Carnegie's success, but without the baggage of a modern point of view. The twelve-year-old appears only for this one question; the next choice introduces a new character. As the lesson continues with a discussion of the popularity of Social Darwinism, and the iteration of the idea in an excerpt from Carnegie's *The Gospel of Wealth* (see below for more information on using documents), students then make this choice:

> **You Decide!** Imagine that you, as a group of Carnegie's workers, approach Andrew Carnegie to ask for a raise. Choose one full-sentence quote from *The Gospel of Wealth* that might be his reply.

In this choice, students are prompted to think about the day's reading from the perspective of the workers, but they are not given many details about the workers' lives other than their economic disparity compared to Carnegie. The lesson continues with the beginnings of the Homestead strike at Carnegie's steel mill in 1892. The workers protested wage cuts; in response, the manager of the mill locked out the workers. The workers, in turn, seized the mill. Students then are given this choice:

> **You Decide!** If you were Andrew Carnegie, how would you respond to either the workers or the manager or both? Why?

Across the three choices, the characters change from one question to the next, and the earlier response from the twelve-year-old hearing about Carnegie's success has no bearing on the later choice that puts the students in Carnegie's shoes. The perspective changes again for the final question at the end of the lesson, when students are prompted to think critically about the lesson's main ideas:

> **You Decide!** Was Carnegie's handling of the Homestead strike an unfortunate mistake, or was it consistent with his beliefs about society and economics? Why?

This prompt allows space for students to consider their own role in responding to historical events; bringing the students' perspective into the discussion can lead to further analysis of the relationship between historical events and present issues.

There are pros and cons to this option for creating characters. Changing the character for each question has the benefit of having all students consider multiple perspectives. Unlike the example in Option 2, where the class was divided into different perspectives, with this method the whole class looks through several lenses in considering an event. Changing characters also helps give equal weight to the opinions of each group involved in an event.

In the Carnegie lesson explained above, some students may be predisposed to agree more easily with either Carnegie or the workers. If they were given the character of only Carnegie or only the workers for the whole lesson, they might not consider the views of the other side very deeply. Being forced to consider all the viewpoints leads students to see how historical actors came to their conclusions. Finally, this format is probably the easiest You Decide lesson to write, because instructors do not have to worry about a decision tree or about how characters interact.

Nevertheless, there are downsides to this method as well. Students have very little emotional connection to a character that they only play for one question. There is no room to develop the character over a series of choices, and the students do not have the opportunity to choose any characteristics. In addition, because the characters change from one question to the next, the choices in earlier decisions do not have any bearing on later decisions, making the format pretty far removed from the Choose Your Own Adventure idea.

Finally, as much as there are benefits to playing the character of a real person (such as Carnegie) as opposed to merely a historically plausible person, the discussion prompts and supporting discussion need to recognize that the students' ideas may not accurately reflect the opinions and actions of the real person. Using primary sources is, therefore, a requirement in employing this format.

No matter which method of creating characters the instructor chooses, historical accuracy must be the paramount concern. Paying close attention to the relevant details for any given time period—such as average marrying age, typical jobs, or even common names—ensures that the characters are historically accurate. If students form an emotional connection to their character, even if that just means remembering the characteristics, it is essential that the character they are remembering helps to educate them about the historical time period.

If the goal is for students to connect to and remember the characters they play, it is tempting to instruct the students to make up the characters on their own. With the right group of students and the right parameters, this can work. The best way to limit silliness and the creation of historically implausible characters is to create some limits to the choices. Another way to keep characters historically accurate and to help the students take the lesson seriously is to require them to write out their choices and hand them in for participation. When students have to justify their choices in writing, they think about them more carefully and keep their character consistent from one choice to the next.

Establishing Decisions

The scenario and the main points of the lesson will help determine where to place You Decide! moments within the lecture. It is generally best to have a You Decide every five to seven minutes. Any longer and students start to tune out or stop thinking about the information from the perspective of their character; any shorter and it is difficult to give enough information to set up a complex choice.

On the other hand, it is also important to avoid overdoing it and using up students' attention with too many small choices before getting to the big decisions that encapsulate the main points of the lesson. Knowing the students and classroom dynamics will determine what works best for the class.[16]

There are several options for how to structure the decisions to ensure that students fully engage. One way to present the choice is as a question that leads to open-ended discussion. For example, consider again this choice from the Andrew Carnegie lesson:

You Decide! If you were Andrew Carnegie, how would you respond to either the workers or the manager or both? Why?

The response is open-ended. Students can choose almost any response as long as they can make the argument that it is consistent with what we know about Andrew Carnegie. Including the *why* question forces students to justify and explain their response. Since students are working together in partners or groups in a You Decide lesson, they have to discuss their response, come to a consensus, and either write down the response or share it with the class. Going through all of these steps helps students refine their answers and check to make sure that they are logical and historically plausible.[17]

Another option for a You Decide choice is for the instructor to provide a multiple-choice list and require students to choose an option and then justify it either verbally or in writing. Consider this example from a U.S. History lesson on the Market Revolution (referenced above). Students craft characters who are eighteen years old and living on their parents' farm in New England. Part way through the lesson, the instructor presents this choice:

You Decide! As a farmer in the Northeast, you can't compete with the grain grown and shipped from the Old Northwest.

Will you . . .

1. Turn your farmland into pasture and start raising livestock?
2. Keep up your farm to grow food for your family and to sell to your closest city and then do industrial outwork?
3. Move to a city to work in a factory and send your pay home to your family?

The purpose of using multiple choice is for the instructor to ensure that the choices are historically accurate. An alternate question, such as the following, gives students too much leeway: "As a farmer in the Northeast, you can't compete with the grain grown and shipped from the Old Northwest. What will you do?" In response, students without significant background knowledge likely will not be able to come up with the range of historically accurate choices presented in the multiple-choice list.

Nevertheless, in some instances, the instructor should create opportunities for students to discover the range of choices available to their character. If the choice contains an essential concept for students to learn, it would be worthwhile to pause, look at sources, allow students to discover the range of choices available to their characters, and then choose. The instructor needs to decide where it is worthwhile to pause and where it is best to keep the momentum going.

One way to dig a little deeper without pausing to look at sources is to have a few students share their decisions, and then the instructor can respond to their choices. For example, with the decision above, if a student shares that they are selecting the first choice the instructor might show maps comparing the physical geography of New England and the Old Northwest; this helps provide more substantial context to the choices.

Having each student group write out their answers is a good way to keep everyone engaged, especially if everyone is a different character, such as a different family member. Writing out responses is also a good option for a large class. On the other hand, it is more engaging (and fun) to hear choices, at least occasionally, and to be able to compare responses across the class.

A multiple-choice You Decide provides a good opportunity to poll the groups about their choice. The instructor can then call on a few students to explain their answers further. Instructors can also poll across character groups. An instructor might ask "How many of you who are women characters chose to vote for Johnson?" and then call on a few students to explain.

Of course, keeping the choices historically accurate is just as important as keeping the scenarios and the characters historically accurate. The next section will explore several strategies for keeping the whole lesson historically accurate and for packing in a surprising number of names, dates, events, and ideas into a You Decide lesson.

Historical Accuracy

While it might seem like all the time needed to create characters and make decisions would take too much time away from covering content in the lesson, in practice, however, it is possible to include a significant amount of specific historical content. Because students are engaged, they are primed to hear, respond to, and remember the content. Between each decision, there are five to seven minutes to move the narrative forward or delve deeply into a particular issue before setting up the next choice. This time can be full of names, dates, and events, and instructors can check students' understanding of the content in how they frame the next decision.

To illustrate, in the You Decide question from the 1960s lesson explained above, where student groups consist of a mother, father, and teenager, the question is sandwiched between significant content discussion. The lesson begins with President John F. Kennedy's assassination. It continues for about seven minutes, going into detail on Lyndon B. Johnson's presidential agenda, the rise of New Conservatives and Barry Goldwater, and the election of 1964. You Decide phrasing for the next choice is purposeful in requiring students to recall the information that the instructor just presented:

You Decide! Who would the parents in your family vote for in 1964? Why? (Remember, the voting age was twenty-one until 1971!)

Students have to remember who the two candidates were. Answering the *why* question also forces students to engage with the ideas that motivated the candidates. If an individual student did not take good notes, their group can help them out.

Another way to include more specific content is to recognize that students pay extra attention to the postdecision "reveal" that explains what characters did historically. With careful planning, those moments can be leveraged to include the most important historical content in the lesson. A You Decide lesson, therefore, can even be used when preparing for a content-heavy test like the Advanced Placement exam. Because students are most attentive to see how historical actors' choices compare to their own character's choices, instructors should capitalize on that peak attentiveness to introduce and reinforce key content.[18]

As an example, the reveal after the You Decide voting decision for 1964, shown above, can lead to an examination of a 1964 election map. The class could also discuss why Johnson beat Goldwater, and then discuss the role Vietnam played in the election and in the beginning of Johnson's second term. The instructor drops in key terms such as "Gulf of Tonkin Resolution," "domino effect," "escalation," and "war of attrition." Since students are curious to see if they are happy with their voting choice and interested to see why real Americans voted similarly or differently from them, they are primed to pay close attention to this specific historical content.

The potency of these reveal moments should not be underestimated. As instructors lead the class through You Decide lessons, students may respond in surprising ways to the reveal moments—cheering, groaning, shaking their heads, or asking questions. This format unlocks a level of engagement that many instructors are constantly striving toward, and instructors should

Using Documents

Another strategic way to ensure that You Decide lessons are both historically accurate and content-rich is to weave primary source analysis into the lesson. There are many ways to incorporate documents into a You Decide lesson. This section will explain a few of these options, but individual instructors will likely come up with many more ways to use documents.

One option is to use the You Decide lesson to set up a document discussion. In this approach, the document is actually the focal point of the lesson (the biggest reveal). Whether students read the document before class or the instructor allocates class time for reading, students will analyze the document from the perspective of their character. This works particularly well if there are multiple characters in the class who will all interpret the documents differently. Instructors can also include a mix of objective and subjective questions in order to fully analyze the document.

Consider these instructions taken from the generation gap lesson, where students are playing the roles of a mother, father, and teenager in the mid-1960s:

Read: National Organization of Women, "Statement of Purpose" (1966, *American Yawp Reader*, excerpt)

Answer the following questions, based on the document:

1. What is the main argument of the "Statement of Purpose"?
2. What particular parts of the document would the mother in your family agree or disagree with? Quote directly from the document and explain.
3. Considering the decisions you have already made, how would the father in your family respond to this document? Explain.
4. The teenager in your family is now twenty years old. Do the ideas in this document reflect the future he or she wants to see? Why or why not? Reference the document specifically.

All of the decisions that the students have made in character leading up to the document discussion will shape the students' response to the document. The mother therefore will think about how she chose to vote in 1964 and the stance she took regarding her teenager's response to the counterculture. Therefore, she will not respond to the NOW document as a generic woman, but as a woman shaped by her biography and the cultural forces of the 1960s.

Bringing this perspective to the document weaves the skills of historical thinking into the document analysis as students see how historical context, intended audience, and author and reader bias all play a role in how a text was read historically. Further, since each student in the group has a unique perspective, they are likely to either disagree with each other's responses or notice different specific information in the document. Discussing the document from multiple perspectives, therefore, leads to deeper engagement.

Another way to use documents is to incorporate them into other You Decide choices. With this option, the class spends less time on the document and uses the document to illustrate a larger trend or show something specific to a historical moment. The goal with this option is not to do an in-depth analysis of the document, but rather to give some evidence to the overall argument of the lesson. Students must read the document beforehand, or the teacher should provide a brief excerpt or something that can be "read" quickly, such as an image.

For example, in a lesson on World War I, students are in character as parents and a teenager or a married couple with an older, live-in parent. In the lesson, the class discusses the definition of *propaganda* and some common uses for propaganda. Then, students look at World War I propaganda posters and respond according to their characters.

In responding to these primary sources, the class will not take the time to investigate the authors of the posters, the specific historical context of their creation, or how they were used. Nevertheless, looking through the posters in character helps to illustrate government use of propaganda to rally citizens as well as how Americans responded to the war differently based on factors such as ethnicity, age, gender, and economic status. To keep that greater analytical depth while also not taking class time to read, instructors can assign students to read the document and answer questions before class; then students have already done the preliminary work of engaging with the document.

Another way to integrate the You Decide format with document analysis is by assigning students to analyze the documents in character for homework. This is similar to the approach taken in the Creating Lives method by Edith Sheffer, where she has students create an avatar that they keep all semester. They then respond to all lectures and readings in character.[19]

The semester-long approach may not be feasible for a survey course or with less-engaged students, but keeping characters from a You Decide class to complete a homework assignment might be more achievable. Some classes might need the original character decision instructions included with the homework; other classes might be able to keep up the characters through several assignments and lessons. The instructor will best be able to judge what scaffolding the class needs to succeed, or they might also realize that asking students to take their characters out of the classroom will not work.

CUSTOMIZE

This chapter has provided specific ways in which to use the You Decide format. Nevertheless, the goal is for instructors to feel inspired and encouraged to make it their own. There are many ways to adapt and adjust these ideas, based on the particularities of both students and content. This section reviews a few things to keep in mind in adapting these ideas to any classroom.

When devising scenarios and setting choices, the instructor bears the responsibility for finding the balance between grabbing students' attention and falling into a scenario that is not historical. In addition, while the Choose Your Own Adventure books sometimes have death as an end point of a decision branch, death is generally not a useful option, especially if there are only two choices. For example, "It is 1608. You are a twenty-two-year-old white, male settler of Jamestown. John Smith has just decided that everyone must work if they want to eat. You Decide! Will you work or will you die?"

Aside from it not being a very interesting choice and the fact that many students will choose to die in the hopes that class will end early, the choice is not particularly historically accurate. There are no known sources from anyone who stoically refused to work so that they could fulfill their choice to die. Even if death is a historically accurate choice—instance, choosing between defending a fort to the death or fleeing in dishonor—the instructor should save it for the last choice of the lesson or use it in a lesson where students take on different characters from one question to another.

There are many ways to customize the use of documents. The You Decide scenario might be a setup to think about authorship and the role of historical context in the creation of any document, including longer historical texts, novels, or even scholarly monographs. With some tweaking, the You Decide format could be used to enter into historiographical debates and to relate primary and secondary sources.

In addition to customizing the scenarios and choices, it is also important to consider when and how often to use a You Decide. Just like any other teaching idea, it will get old and boring if it is used every day. A good rule of thumb is to use it rarely enough that it provides a change of pace but frequently enough to not have to reintroduce the idea and explain all the instructions again. Using it not more than once a week for a class that meets three times a week works well. For a class that meets every day, instructors should use it no more than twice a week and/or not more than three times in two weeks.

CONCLUSION

In considering how to balance instruction in historical thinking with content knowledge, the You Decide approach offers an active-learning solution that works for many different topics and class sizes. By having students live out the ideas of contingency and choice, they see firsthand how historical context shaped the experience of people in the past. Rather than viewing history as a narrative of inevitability, students wrestle with making historically plausible choices.

This chapter outlined several different ways to create You Decide lessons, and instructors can customize further depending on the topic and students. Some general rules to keep in mind: (1) topics that include several decisions moments work best for a You Decide scenario, (2) instructors should consider how much input they want students to have in creating their You Decide characters, (3) the instructor needs to maintain strict historical accuracy in the decisions and characters, as well as the rest of the lesson, and (4) the reveal after a choice is a peak student attention moment and instructors should leverage it to achieve learning goals.

Above all, instructors should own the method for themselves and develop it further to engage their students. In his book *Super Courses: The Future of Teaching and Learning*, Ken Bain concisely argues, "If students have thought about meaning and implications, if they have used information and ideas to solve problems and built rich associations with concepts that matter to them, they are most likely to understand deeply—and remember what they comprehend."[20] The You Decide approach sets students up to attain this goal.

NOTES

1. R. A. Montgomery, *Journey Under the Sea* (1978; repr., Waitsfield: Chooseco, 2005), 2.

2. Leslie Jamison, "The Enduring Allure of Choose Your Own Adventure Books," *The New Yorker*, September 12, 2022.

3. Kathryn Ciancia and Edith Sheffer, "Creating Lives: Fictional Characters in the History Classroom," *Perspectives on History*, October 2013, https://www.historians.org/publications-and-directories/perspectives-on-history/october-2013/creating-lives-fictional-characters-in-the-history-classroom.

4. Thomas Andrews and Flannery Burke, "What Does It Mean to Think Historically?" *Perspectives on History*, January 2007, https://www.historians.org/publications-and-directories/perspectives-on-history/january-2007/what-does-it-mean-to-think-historically. Lendol Calder and Tracy Steffes refine these ideas in arguing that "today's students should develop a deep understanding of history as an interpretive account, the relationship of past and present, historical evidence, complex

causality, and historical significance." Lendol Calder and Tracy Steffes, "Measuring College Learning in History," in *Improving Quality in American Higher Education: Learning Outcomes and Assessments for the 21st Century*, ed. Richard Arum, Josipa Roksa, and Amanda Cook (San Francisco: John Wiley & Sons, 2016), 37. The You Decide approach particularly emphasizes history as an interpretive account and complex causality. Similarly, Susannah Walker and Gustavo Carrera note that "the last two decades or more have seen some significant changes in the teaching of U.S. history at undergraduate and high school levels . . . . A lot of this work advocates discipline-based training and the practice of historical thinking skills, which . . . encourages students to actively seek understanding of the past rather than to passively receive knowledge of it." Susannah Walker and Gustavo Carrera, "Developing a Signature Pedagogy for the High School U.S. History Survey: A Case Study," *The History Teacher* 51, no. 1 (2017): 66.

5. Hartmut Blank and Steffen Nestler, "Perceiving Events as Both Inevitable and Unforeseeable in Hindsight: The Leipzig Candidacy for the Olympics," *British Journal of Social Psychology* 45, no. 1 (2006): 150.

6. See also Ina von der Beck, Ulrike Cress, and Aileen Oeberst, "Is There Hindsight Bias without Real Hindsight? Conjectures Are Sufficient to Elicit Hindsight Bias," *Journal of Experimental Psychology: Applied* 25, no. 1 (August 2018): 88–99, https://doi.org/10.1037/xap0000185.

7. Andrews and Burke, "What Does It Mean to Think Historically?"

8. Facing History and Ourselves, accessed June 13, 2023, https://www.facinghistory.org/.

9. "Guiding Principles for Choices Content Development," Choices Program Brown University, accessed June 13, 2023, https://www.choices.edu/about/guiding-principles/.

10. See also Julie Anne Sweet, "Making History Come Alive: The Boston Massacre Trials," *The History Teacher* 54 no. 3 (May 2021): 509–38.

11. This approach helps to examine concepts more deeply, rather than a traditional lecture that can breeze through terms and definitions without much development or discussion of examples. Daniel Moreau and Jonathan Smith note that "the conceptualization approach leads to a tendency . . . to favor steps that help to more quickly define the targeted concept—to the detriment of their application to examples and their linking with other concepts." Daniel Moreau and Jonathan Smith, "Teachers Helping Their Students Think Historically . . . at Last?," *The History Teacher* 54 no. 4 (August 2021): 749.

12. I developed the root idea behind using characters while reading David Gooblar's argument about constructivism: "If we accept that students learn best when they take part in the kinds of activities in which they hold their preconceptions up to the light and revise them, then we must adjust our focus." David Gooblar, *The Missing Course: Everything They Never Taught You about College Teaching* (Cambridge, MA: Harvard University Press, 2019), 21. Students may have preconceived ideas about "the sixties" but looking at the time period from the perspective of a historically plausible person forces students to revised their preconceptions.

13. For further discussion of using small group work as the central focus in the history classroom, see Carole Srole, Christopher Endy, and Birte Pfleger, "Active Learning in History Survey Courses: The Value of 'In-Class' Peer Mentoring," *The History Teacher* 51, no. 1 (2017): 89–102.

14. Putting students in a "family" or other type of related groups mimics many of the benefits of a Jigsaw activity in which "each student has an important role in the learning of the class, which promotes positive interdependence." Claire Howell Major, Michael S. Harris, and Todd Zakrajsek, *Teaching for Learning: 101 Intentionally Designed Educational Activities to Put Students on the Path to Success* (New York: Routledge, 2016), 110.

15. The Reacting to the Past pedagogy (discussed in a later chapter) is built on the benefits of creating an emotional connection to historical actors. See Mark Carnes, *Minds on Fire: How Role Immersion Games Transform College* (Cambridge, MA: Harvard University Press, 2014).

16. The scholarship that supports incorporating decision moments is the idea that "you learn better when you wrestle with new problems before being shown the solution, rather than the other way around." We see this easily in math classes, where watching the teacher solve a problem is a far cry from being faced with a problem set yourself. Similarly in history, hearing the results of people's choices told in a seamless narrative removes all of the problems that historical actors had to work through. Mimicking those problems in the classroom and having students make choices in historical scenarios helps them learn the history more deeply. Peter C. Brown, Henry L. Roediger III, and Mark A. McDaniel, *Making It Stick: The Science of Successful Learning* (Cambridge, MA: Belknap Press, 2014), 226.

17. This approach also helps students become "adaptive experts" by finding solutions to problems they haven't seen before. Because the solutions need to be historically plausible but are otherwise open-ended, students can come up with creative answers and solutions, which helps them think through the historical context more deeply. See discussion of adaptive experts in Ken Bain, *Super Courses: The Future of Teaching and Learning* (Princeton: Princeton University Press, 2021).

18. This finding regarding increased attention during "reveal" moments tracks with recent studies on students' attention in the classroom, namely, that, as James Lang notes, "change and variety" throughout a lesson helps to cultivate attention. Lang highlights researchers who found "not only that student attention perked up during these changes in format from lecture to active learning, but that the reverse was also true: student attention was heightened during the lecture segments following an active learning experience." James M. Lang, *Distracted: Why Students Can't Focus and What You Can Do about It* (New York: Basic Books, 2020), 152.

19. Ciancia and Sheffer, "Creating Lives."

20. Bain, *Super Courses*, 74.

Chapter 2

History Lab

In popular culture, historians are often depicted as exciting adventurers and treasure hunters, able to expertly interpret evidence and discover clues—think *Indiana Jones* or *National Treasure*. All too often, however, history and social studies classrooms are devoid of interest and excitement and are more similar to the excruciatingly dull History of Magic classes in Harry Potter, where a ghostly teacher drones on and on, putting students to sleep.

Historians know that the process of historical discovery is exciting and interesting. The thrill of not knowing what they will find next or how it will fit into everything else can make hours of research fly by. Implementing "history labs" is one way to bring the thrill of doing history into the classroom. In this format, rather than giving students heavily curated documents or document excerpts, students instead examine and sift through a set of primary sources, analyze and evaluate them as a whole, dig deeper into a smaller set, and make an argument derived from their discoveries.

Instead of starting with an argument or a statement and then cherry-picking facts and document excerpts to support it, the archive is preeminent, and the argument flows from discovery. This approach allows even beginner students to experience how history is constructed and why it is intriguing—and even fun! A sample history lab is included at the end of the chapter.

IN THEORY

History labs build on the work of a number of historians and educators who share a frustration for the lack of historical discovery in the day-to-day lessons of many lower-level courses. Nancy Shoemaker transformed her survey course into a semester-long history lab and was pleased when her students "did the work of real historians and along the way discovered the pleasures of the hunt, felt exhilaration when new information transformed understanding, and realized the satisfaction of piecing together bits of evidence from the documents to tell a coherent story."[1]

Shoemaker's class worked together to research and write about a single historical event. Many history teachers may not have that luxury. State tests, licensure exams, and general education requirements demand that our students develop at least a general knowledge of a set time period. Still, the possibilities of capturing the essence of Shoemaker's approach are readily available.

ShawnaKim Lowey-Ball asserts that the process of historical discovery—with all its inefficiencies—is essential before students make an argument, noting, "We don't really form our arguments—or even discover our true research subjects—until we've sat with our documents and found the interesting truths within them."[2] It is easy to want to hurry students along well-worn paths of discovery, but we must remember that the paths and the discovery process are brand-new to them. Documents or even document collections that established historians can summarize at a glance are fresh to novice students, and we must not rob them of the engaging pleasure of making discoveries for themselves.

This approach works within a larger emphasis on "doing history." Many educators have developed their own methods for inviting students to do the real work of historians, rather than sit in class as passive receptors of established knowledge. Joel Sipress and David Voelker provide this definition of doing history: "Students directly enter a contested discourse in which they produce their own judgments and argue for them on the basis of historical evidence."[3] It is the "directly enter" part of the process that is realized in a history lab assignment. Rather than having the experience be heavily mitigated by the teacher, students themselves learn how to manage the complexities of working with an archive and develop a position they can defend based on the evidence they find.

The approach is also informed by the concept known as "far transfer." Christine Baron utilized this approach in creating lab-based experiences for educators visiting historic sites. She notes that "students should be able to take what they learn in one setting and use or transfer it to novel settings."[4] A lab experience that focuses on skills more than content has more possibilities for deep learning and far transfer. Ideally, students will take their investigative experience gained through history labs and use it not only for history research papers but also for other tasks such as evaluating current news stories or seeking a variety of perspectives before making a choice.

Carla Vecchiola developed a method for "doing history" in her online courses. She discovered that she could facilitate student engagement with primary sources by directing them to explore and analyze databases or collections of primary sources. She found that "direct access to primary source databases resulted in a class culture of active learning."[5] Vecchiola does not specifically mandate which sources in a collection students should examine; instead, she allows students to work through and explore the set themselves and share their discoveries with the class.

Vecchiola found that this student-centered approach worked particularly well in an online course. Her students were more engaged on discussion boards than they had been when she was more heavily curating the course material. Students were enthusiastic about sharing their discoveries and comparing their findings with fellow classmates. Vecchiola notes that this approach is particularly well-adapted for an online class because of the availability of online repositories of primary and archival sources.[6]

The history lab approach, therefore, builds on all this work to provide students with an authentic archival experience and the opportunity to do history. By using group work, digital repositories, and immediate instructor feedback, students experience a laboratory culture of discovery, hypothesis testing, and trial and error.

IN PRACTICE

While there are many benefits to a full-semester history lab course or a hands-on lab experience at a historic site, it is possible to capture the benefits of working directly with archives to craft arguments and gain transferable historical skills in a traditional classroom setting. With some adjustment, history labs are possible even in large classes. Incorporating weekly or biweekly history labs into a history course can teach students the importance of archival work while also maintaining the content goals of the course.

In a history lab assignment, teachers direct students to investigate and make an argument based on a digital archive. The instructors provide research and analysis questions, but the questions are open-ended, with a variety of possible answers. However, a history lab assignment differs significantly from a traditional document-based essay assignment.

Rather than working through a set of curated and excerpted documents, students work together to search through a large set of historical sources to find stories, connections, and mysteries and then piece together responses to prompts that instruct them to investigate deeply and form an argument. This approach is meant to foster an authentic research experience that mirrors the work that historians do, while taking into account the constraints of time and resources.

Choosing Topics

What topics make for an engaging and worthwhile history lab? In addition to meeting course learning goals, instructors should consider three interrelated factors: an accessible source set (discussed in "Finding the Archive" section), topics that activate and expand prior knowledge, and topics that are complex enough to warrant group work.

The best topics provide a closer look at a subject that is already part of the class, either thematically or chronologically. For example, in a U.S. History survey class, a history lab about John Brown's raid on Harper's Ferry and the ensuing trial will likely fit into thematic discussions about slavery and sectionalism or chronological discussions about the road to the Civil War. In contrast, a World History since 1500 survey might not provide enough context about the particularities of abolition debates in the United States in 1859 to make John Brown's raid a useful topic. Students need enough historical content knowledge to have some sense of what they are looking at when they survey the sources.

Additionally, the topic must be complex enough that it will lead to sorting and sifting through the source set. A set with only a few sources will require that students use all of the sources. While this curated approach works for other assignments, it circumvents the point of a history lab, which is to mimic the excitement and unknowns of searching through an archive, with sources varying in relevance, depending on the goals and the research question. For example, three letters from John Brown would not give students enough to work with, even if the letters are the only three that Brown wrote on a particular day and are therefore a complete "set."

Some topics that could work for a U.S. History survey course include daily life in Jamestown, Virginia; runaway slave advertisements; the journals of Lewis and Clark; or abolitionist writings in *The Liberator*.[7] The topic ideas point to the centrality of the archive or source set, rather than a predetermined content goal.

Finding the Archive

The goal is for the set of documents that students are examining to be fairly uncurated, given the abilities of students and the time constraints of the class. Finding a set of documents that is relevant to the topic while also striking the right balance between being challenging but not too challenging is one of the most important steps in the setup phase. The question arises: Why an archive? Why not a set of documents in a reader? Or, why not have students search the internet for primary sources?[8]

A document reader is too curated to give students a taste of the excitement and frustration of archival work; they must have the opportunity to sift through sources that may or may not be relevant. Within this goal, there is still plenty of space to narrow down the set. Consider a few examples and why they work particularly well:

1. Newspapers: There are many online repositories of newspapers, and instructors can narrow these down in a variety of ways. For a history lab about John Brown's raid on Harper's Ferry, Virginia, the instructor can present an archive of newspapers that published editorials about John Brown's raid.[9] The benefits of this set are that all of the articles are relevant while presenting contrasting views, students are looking at images of the actual newspapers, and the newspapers are from all around the country. In addition, students do not have to spend time searching for individual newspapers or trying to figure out the names of the newspapers to search for.

Students still have to do the work of sifting through the dozens of newspapers available to find a smaller subset to examine more fully. A group of four students scanning through newspapers for ten minutes can work through a few dozen fairly quickly, especially if they have been instructed on how to work efficiently together.

2. Personal journals or diaries: Collected repositories of journals or diaries related to a single event or time period are similarly useful. Although most online repositories will have transcriptions of the diaries, rather than page images, many archives will have sample images of the actual document. While spending time deciphering handwriting is not feasible in a short class period, the availability of full-text, searchable collections of diaries and journals makes it possible to compare events or dates across several journals. For example, students can search across trail diaries from travelers on the Oregon and California trails to compare how they prepared to leave or how they viewed a specific location.[10]

Now consider a few examples of source sets that do not work as well:

1. Curated document sets: Websites such as the Digital Public Library of America or the Library of Congress offer curated sets of documents on a wide variety of topics. The sets include many different types of documents: book excerpts, pamphlets, images, songs, and the like. The sets are tied together based on the topic, but the documents are not necessarily related in any other way. They were not all created by the same person or at the same time and they are not all the same type of document. While this type of source set is a marvelous resource for a variety of other activities, it does not work for a history lab because it is too curated.

Sources that are preselected for their relevance deny students the opportunity and challenge of sifting for themselves. Students cannot make serendipitous discoveries while skimming through an archive, because the documents are presented outside of their original context. For example, while a single song about the Fifteenth Amendment is an interesting source, a collection of political songs published in the three years after the Civil War ended or a collection of songs by one author—some political and some not—is a more useful set for a history lab assignment.

2. Document excerpts: It can be tempting to simply give students the most relevant excerpts from documents. Full of ellipses and brackets, these document sets might seem to be the most efficient way to teach students to use documents to support an argument. There are several pitfalls to this approach, however. First, a heavily curated and excerpted list of documents flattens out history and makes it dull. Handing students the documents removes the elements of search and discovery and can give the illusion that the excerpts on the list are the full primary source record of the event.

Document excerpts also remove the necessity of students deciding which documents are relevant and why. Although teachers might feel like they are doing their students a favor, an edited set takes documents out of their context, which can lead to students misinterpreting the documents altogether. Finally, the lack of efficiency is part of the point. If students learn early on that documents do not simply arrive prepackaged, they are more likely to be prepared to search deeply when doing their own research projects.

Group Roles and Work

A history lab assignment is predicated on utilizing group work and peer instruction. While it is often best practice to avoid assigning work to a group that could be done more efficiently and effectively alone, some assignments—particularly those that involve complex problems—are better completed with a group. Students receive the benefits of peer instruction as they struggle together to work through the archive and develop their argument.[11]

For the group work to be effective, it is necessary to assign a specific and clear role to each group member. Since the document set is not highly curated, the teacher needs to put in extra effort to get groups working quickly and efficiently. This "formal cooperative learning" involves more initial setup from the instructor, but once students learn the basic format, the assignment can be used throughout the semester with minimal setup time.[12]

While there are many ways to divide up roles, the main roles needed for a history lab are the following:

1. Leader: The leader keeps the group on task and working through the assignment. This person keeps track of time and assigns tasks as needed. The leader assists with researching and answering questions.

2. Writer: The writer drafts the group's answers to the questions and incorporates the research into the written response. Having one writer keeps the

group working together on the same task, rather than trying to write individual, disconnected responses. The writer assists with research as needed.

3. Contextualizer: The contextualizer relates the research and the answers to the larger historical context. This person carefully reads all provided background material and makes connections to other information discussed in class. The contextualizer makes sure that the answer includes specific facts and information and ensures that the answer is historically accurate.

While there are many other roles that instructors could assign, the ideal group size for a history lab is three people; the assignment provides enough work for three students to work hard but not have to rush. In addition, all three students participate in the work of researching, so they equally participate in the project's main learning goal. Nevertheless, groups of four might be more feasible, especially in very large classes where the grading load is heavy. In the case of four group members, include a specific Researcher role:

4. Researcher: The researcher takes the lead in sifting through sources and deciding which documents to focus on. The researcher has a good holistic sense of the set's content and guides the group in making connections among documents.

Teachers should instruct students to divide up the roles and note the division on the group document. While it might seem like an overly controlling step to insist that students divide up the work in this particular way, much of the resistance to group work comes from students not sharing the work equally or from the group wasting time getting started. Clear roles eliminate some of the initial stress that comes from group work and ensures that all students will benefit from the learning opportunity.[13]

It is important to explain to students that history lab assignments benefit from a group work structure. Students should use their collective knowledge to answer questions and challenge each other's interpretations; this approach leads to more developed answers to questions than would result from students working alone. In addition, because students are working with a large set of documents, they must discuss and decide with each other regarding which documents are important, what themes they are noticing across the documents, and how the documents relate to each other. Much of the assignment's deep learning comes from that discussion.

For example, in a history lab that tasks students with evaluating newspaper editorials about John Brown's raid on Harper's Ferry, students can use their collective knowledge of the event to put the editorials in chronological order. As students read the editorials, they can compare editorials from the North and South and, as the conversation develops, realize that geographic location was not the most important factor in determining whether an editorial would be for or against the raid, though it did play some role.

Because students must have a conversation in order to complete the tasks, they benefit from the unique perspectives and interpretations of each group member. Even as they read the same document, each student will have different perceptions, insights, and connections. Having a conversation about the documents then allows students to benefit from group members' unique perspectives while being able to correct each other's inaccuracies. It is critical that the instructor explain these benefits and guide students through having effective conversations, particularly for the first history lab in the course.

Source Analysis

Vecchiola devised two steps to encourage her students to analyze sources deeply. The first step is to choose five or six documents to examine as a subset. The second step is to choose one of the six to examine in more detail.[14] Vecchiola then included several prompts for students to respond to, based on their chosen document subsets. The brilliance of these instructions is that they can be adapted to almost any type of archive and provide building blocks for other types of assignments.

The steps are also easily adaptable to many course learning goals. For learning goals related to primary source analysis skills, the prompts can focus on questions of authorship, audience, purpose, and significance. For learning goals related to content acquisition, the prompts can focus on building historical knowledge, the importance of chronology, and how the documents or artifacts relate to the relevant historical context.

Consider this example for a prompt about the Smithsonian Institution's online artifact collection related to Maya civilization from 1000 to 1550 CE (67 objects).[15] A prompt focused on building historical knowledge could look like this:

> Investigate the Sources: Working together, choose five or six different artifacts, read the information about each one, and look at the larger images, clicking through the pictures if there is more than one. *Investigation Question: From your overall look at five or six artifacts and the provided context, what can you learn about life in the Maya civilization during this time period? (five sentences minimum).* Resist making broad generalizations (example: "All Maya people were religious."); instead, try to answer narrowly and specifically. What did they seem to value? Were these objects only functional or did they serve other purposes? What sort of person might use or make these objects? Where were the objects made? and so on. Discuss the five or six objects as a general group, not each object in depth.[16]

This prompt builds historical knowledge by instructing students to investigate who the Maya were as a society, what they made and valued, where they lived and the location's effect on their lives, and when these artifacts were made and how they fit into the larger chronology. Students will not gain full knowledge of all of these points, but they will get a glimpse into how historical knowledge is constructed. Instructors can refer back to the source set in later lessons to reinforce the content knowledge.

To compare, a prompt focused on primary source analysis could look like this:

> Investigate the Sources: Working together, choose five or six different artifacts, read the information about each one, and look at the larger images, clicking through the pictures if there is more than one. *Investigation Question: From your overall look at five or six artifacts and the provided context, to what extent is analyzing these objects a useful way to understand Maya civilization? (five sentences minimum).* Use the objects to determine as much as you can about these questions: Who made these objects? Who was the intended audience? When were the objects made and how do they relate to what we know about Maya civilization? In what ways can historians use these objects to understand Maya society? What are the limits of these objects as primary sources?

This prompt teaches historical source analysis skills by challenging students to think about the artifacts as evidence for historical arguments. By not only evaluating what the source is but also how historians can use it, students see how historians move from historical sources to historical arguments. This prompt also helps students start to think about their own arguments relating to the source set.

After students gain an overall sense of the source set as a whole, the next step is to focus more closely on one document or artifact. This step continues the peer instruction as students decide which document to examine more closely and discuss its characteristics and significance together. The point is not to simply list interesting facts about the document; rather, students should use their more detailed examination to practice making an evidence-based argument. Because students are only examining one item, the assignment's format forces them to make a specific argument that they can support with their in-depth reading of one source, instead of a generalized argument with only superficial support.

To continue the example of the Maya civilization history lab, consider this prompt:

> Make an Argument: Choose one artifact out of the five or six you looked at, and paste a picture of it in your answer. *Based on this object and the secondary source historical context, to what extent were the Maya a complex society?* Answer the question with an argument and discuss the significance of your object in depth. Connect the object to the relevant historical context. Use these

questions to guide your thinking: What aspects of Maya society does this object help us understand? Why? How does this object connect to other aspects of Maya society?

By keeping the scope limited, the assignment sets students up to be able to make an evidence-based argument and to use the evidence within its appropriate historical context. Looking at the set as a whole, then a smaller subset, then just one item allows students to build their knowledge over the course of the assignment and then use that knowledge to make an argument.

Immediate Feedback

The key to a successful history lab is the inclusion of immediate feedback. Similar to how a scientific lab report is an analysis of results and outcomes, a history lab must have that element of knowing if the answers are accurate or not. In the historical discipline, conversation and critique among historians serves the same purposes as measurements and observations in a scientific lab—both give feedback on whether the hypothesis is correct.

To replicate the immediate feedback of a completed experiment, the instructor serves as an expert peer reviewer who critiques the use and interpretation of evidence and the accuracy of the argument. As student groups finish answering a question, they call the instructor over to read and critique the response. Students then adjust their answer based on the review.

This immediate feedback is different from postclass grading in several ways. First, the instructor critiques the answer as soon as the group completes it and gives suggestions for revision. Students can then ask clarifying questions and revise their answer based on the feedback. The group does not receive a grade on their first attempt but rather on the revised answer.

Second, while students either do not read feedback on graded work or cannot do anything retroactively in response to the feedback on graded work, immediate feedback extends the learning opportunity for students and helps to close the learning loop.[17] In addition, the chance to revise and receive full credit motivates students to work hard on the first attempt to save time on revision. The emphasis moves away from rushing through the work to be "done" quickly and toward making a valid, in-depth argument.

Third, the process gives students the opportunity to do the work of real historians, who write as part of a conversation and revise their arguments based on informed peer critique. By asking questions relating to evidence or clarity of argument, instructors give students the chance to reflect on how the "historical community" (represented by the instructor) would respond to their argument. The goal, therefore, is not to get a grade, but rather to make a plausible, evidence-based argument—that is, to "do history."

Immediate feedback has benefits for the instructor as well. Giving feedback in class cuts down on grading time outside of class. Unless a group chooses not to revise their answer in response to the teacher's feedback, all students should leave class with a grade of 100 percent. For a formative assessment where the goal is content and skills acquisition, the main purpose of the grade is to induce students to complete the assignment, not to measure whether their first attempt at answering was correct.

After class, the instructor does not need to read the assignments again but instead simply enters the grades. From the instructor perspective, it is more satisfying to give students feedback that they can act on at once, rather than wasting time on feedback that has very little instructional usefulness. Even if the answer is satisfactory, the instructor can briefly explain to students why it is correct or what they did particularly well.

Giving feedback on the answer to the first question before students answer the second question also helps students take that feedback into their second response. If the first answer lacked evidentiary support, and students revise the answer, they can be aware of that requirement when writing the second answer and adjust accordingly. As Ken Bain highlights in *Super Courses: The Future of Teaching and Learning*, "The aim of feedback . . . should be to leave someone eager to get back to work."[18]

How can a teacher give immediate feedback in a relatively short period of time, especially to a large number of students? Because instructors know what they are looking for and what a satisfactory answer looks like—essentially carrying the rubric in their heads—scanning each answer and giving feedback generally only takes about one minute. A class of thirty divided into ten groups results in about ten minutes of feedback on the first question and ten minutes on the second—even less if students have learned from their first response.

This approach leaves plenty of time to give extra feedback and support to groups that need it or walk around the room answering questions and correcting steps in the process. To avoid a rush at the end of class, the instructor can begin responding to answers that are close to being completed during the last ten minutes of class.

For a class larger than thirty students, where a teaching assistant is not available, feedback can be handled differently. By including time instructions for each step in the lab and tasking the group leaders with keeping track of time, the instructor can pause the session after most students have completed the first question and spend a few minutes reviewing a good answer and a poor answer and giving students tips to revise. The group leader can then lead the revision process, and the instructor is available to help groups that need more feedback. For the second question, the instructor can display a rubric or specific grading criteria and task the group leader with grading the answer.

While the instructor of a large class might need to spend extra time on grading because she has not seen all of the responses, giving students some feedback and instructions on how and when to revise should still provide most of the benefits of immediate feedback. Even if students are inclined to grade their answers at 100 percent, the chance to revise before submitting should improve the quality of the answers for all but the least motivated groups.

Potential Pitfalls

There are several ways in which a history lab can lose its effectiveness. First, because students are encountering a large set of documents that cannot all be read in the time allotted, they may become overwhelmed and have trouble getting started or effectively communicating with each other regarding which documents to choose. This pitfall is especially threatening for the first few times that a class completes a history lab. This problem can be mitigated for some classes simply by taking extra time to review the instructions or completing the first lab as a whole class under guidance from the instructor. Other classes would benefit from accessing a more limited set of documents for the first lab.

In the Maya civilization example discussed above, rather than sending students to a collection of sixty-seven documents, the instructor could narrow down the dates from 1500 to 1550 only, resulting in a set of just twenty-three documents.[19] This still gives the benefits of a complete source set but takes away some of the necessity for sorting and deciding. As students become more comfortable with the process, the instructor can give them larger or more advanced sets of documents.

An effective group leader can also be the key to a group moving through a large set of documents efficiently. It might be worthwhile, therefore, to give more specific guidance to leaders or handpick the leaders. Instructor intervention and guidance during the first steps helps groups keep moving as well.

Another potential problem is that students might not recognize the significance and/or meaning of the documents or artifacts. To combat this, instructors need to equip students with adequate context. Homework or class activities in the days leading up to the history lab can be focused on providing the context needed so that students can effectively interpret the source set. For example, understanding the gender and religious structures of the Maya is a critical foundation for interpreting Maya artifacts. While it is useful to provide contextual secondary sources within the history lab, it is less overwhelming for students if those sources are reinforcing prior knowledge, not providing new content.

Focusing on providing context for an upcoming history lab might mean sacrificing some "content coverage" time, but it is repaid in the acquisition of skills and the depth of knowledge related to the history lab topics, and in that sense, history labs should be used strategically to teach material that the instructor deems most important. Having adequate historical context also means students will recognize meaning and significance in their initial scans of the source set. For example, spending time discussing the importance of music to Maya society and culture helps students recognize the significance of a whistling jar in a list of various Maya artifacts.[20]

Students also might interpret the documents or artifacts inaccurately or draw conclusions that are inconsistent with the source set as a whole. This is where immediate feedback is critical to effective learning. As the instructor circulates, they can intercede when students are misinterpreting. In addition, quickly scanning the answers and giving additional instruction and feedback ensures that student errors are corrected before the lab experience is complete.

History Labs and Research Papers

The benefits of a history lab extend beyond *introducing* students to archival work and how historians do history. Students should recognize—perhaps with some prompting—that the skills for completing a history lab transfer to successfully completing a research paper. In a high school or lower-level college class, the instructor can make this connection explicit by using a history lab as the first step in a research paper.

It is not simply the skills of analyzing documents that students need to transfer over to their research process. There are three key takeaways from a history lab that will make the research process more effective and the resulting research papers more accurate, convincing, and thorough.

First, rather than cherry-picking documents that fit their argument, students learn to examine the sources first and then form their argument. In the age of search engines, students can be tempted to only find out-of-context documents that fit their preformed arguments. Rather than wandering through an archive and allowing the argument to form naturally through wide reading and examination, students can quickly assemble a list of random documents that seem to support an argument. A history lab, however, helps students become comfortable with examining large sets of documents and then making arguments based on a reading of the set as a whole.

Second, as students work together in a group, they learn that other people see documents differently. To stick with the example of the Maya civilization collection, a student interested in warfare and weaponry might be drawn to examine the differences between the "bifacial tool/projectile points" in the source set while another student will scan past those as he is drawn toward the various "human figures." As the instructor circulates through the room, she will overhear students saying, "What really caught my eye was . . ." or "I'm interested in X, so I started looking at . . . " Students' ability to verbalize how they are interpreting the archive and to recognize why and how others interpret it differently is an important skill to transfer to a research project. In most cases, it is the instructor's responsibility to make those connections explicit.

Third, a history lab also forces students to make connections across documents, rather than discussing sources individually. This skill, if reinforced by the instructor, helps novice researchers avoid the "one paragraph, one document" problem. Because students are having a conversation about the source set, they practice the skill of putting the sources in conversation with each other. The student who was drawn to the "bifacial tool/projectile points" must recognize—perhaps with some prodding from the instructor or group—that he cannot eliminate the "human figures" from his group's appraisal of Maya civilization. Introducing this complexity at the lower levels makes for more robust research skills at the higher levels.

CUSTOMIZE

There are many ways in which instructors can make the history lab assignment their own. From shifting the sources used to using physical collections to extending the length or scope of the history lab, instructors should consider how to make the project most effective for their students' learning.

While the history lab focuses on historical (primary) sources, instructors might choose to emphasize historiography by pairing the archive with the conversations historians are having about the sources. The history lab questions could then task students to examine both the sources and the arguments that historians make about the sources, before students make their own contributions to the discussion. That type of lesson might need to extend over two class periods in order to avoid students rushing through the assignment.[21]

As digital archives continue to develop, expand, and become more accessible, the possibilities for history lab source sets will continue to grow. One way to customize the history lab approach is to rely on data culled from primary sources, rather than focusing on the sources themselves. A data-based approach significantly widens the amount of primary source information that students encounter and shows the benefits of digital history.

For example, the SlaveVoyages website utilizes and gives access to the records of over ninety thousand enslaved captives over the course of thirty-six thousand voyages across the Atlantic Ocean. The possibilities for research, modeling, collating, and customizing are endless. Yet, at the same time, the website makes the data accessible and manageable for students. A series of history labs using the data could be linked to form the foundation for a unit on many aspects of the trade in enslaved persons.[22]

Similarly, enhancements in visualization technology make three-dimensional objects more accessible than ever. For example, the David Rumsey Map Collection through Cartography Associates seeks to present ancient maps with the precision and accessibility of Google Earth. Being able to see and digitally manipulate ancient understandings of the globe opens up new possibilities for researching and comparing historical maps. As augmented and virtual reality technology continues to develop, students will gain even greater access to these maps. While a history lab cannot come close to examining the over 117,000 maps and related images available, the sophisticated searchable database creates opportunities to limit and customize the source set, all while keeping the focus on cartography.[23]

Digital and online resources provide a wealth of information that previous generations of historians only dreamed of. Being able to sort through the high-quality images from the Smithsonian or the British Museum from the classroom is a significant advantage over seeing one or two images in a book or even transcriptions of archival documents. Despite all the advantages of digital access, in classes where part of the instructor's job is to cultivate a love of history and impart the dynamism of archival work, hands-on experience with physical objects can provide a welcome change of pace and enhance the learning experience for students.

Many universities have physical archives and special collections, and some archivists may be willing to bring a selection to a high school classroom. The same is true for local historical societies or libraries. It is also important to not overlook physical archives from other sources. A friend with an interesting collection of similar items may be willing to lend their archive to be the basis of a history lab. A collection of classic toys from the 1950s, memorabilia from the Vietnam War, or a collection of vintage vinyl could all serve as an archive worthy of interrogation. Even something as simple as a stack of old yearbooks can spark questions and foster in-depth research.

The format for a physical archive history lab can be the same as for a digital collection, except that the instructor needs to give extra time for examining sources. When the documents or objects are physically piled up in front of the students, it is easy for them to get sidetracked by looking at old pictures or leafing through newspapers or deciphering the cursive script of hundred-year-old love letters. This "wandering through the archive" should be encouraged (within reason), not curtailed.[24] Having a physical archive history lab span two class periods or moving part of the assignment to online group discussion boards for homework can help the class carve out enough time to experience the archive more fully.

In thinking about the best way to deploy history lab assignments within a unit, there are several options. The instructor could schedule weekly history labs, perhaps in large lecture courses that have weekly recitations, or history labs can be scheduled more randomly according to the content. The benefit of the approach is that once students understand how it works, they can quickly get to work without having to receive new instruction.

Another idea is to expand the history lab to a unit-long activity. That method would allow for a much deeper dive into a set of sources. It could work particularly well for archives that are a mix of digital and physical resources. Of course, the steps and questions would need to be expanded to fit the learning goals of the unit, and instructors could expect a more developed final product at the end of a unit-length history lab.

A history lab can also give structure for a field trip to a historic site. Either working with a curator or director or doing some advanced scouting, the instructor can determine how students will physically interact with historical artifacts and develop analysis questions based on the artifacts. Instructors can also challenge students to make an argument, either based on their experience of doing the work of historical interpretation or based on their close examination of artifacts or documents.

CONCLUSION

A history lab brings students into archival work while considering the restraints of time and resources. The purpose of a history lab is not simply to allow students to work with primary sources; instead, the goal is to give students the thrill of discovery and the intrigue of complex and puzzling mysteries. By presenting students with a complete source set (within reason), instructors take a hands-off approach to encourage active student engagement.

This approach follows the work of scholars who seek to include students in the process of historical discovery. Many teaching scholars try to foster a culture of "doing history" in their classrooms, and the history lab outlined in this chapter adds to that attempt. In addition, some scholars have found creative ways to use digital historical source archives that allow researchers to search, sort, and categorize documents and artifacts.

In practice, instructors can follow a template that includes finding a topic and source set, crafting "investigation" and "argument" questions according to learning goals, instructing groups on working together effectively, and providing immediate feedback in class. This template can be adapted to many topics and source sets, as long as the spirit of discovery is the motivation.

The assignment can also be customized by using physical and/or digital collections or visiting historic sites. In addition, adding secondary sources can change the history lab to meet different learning goals.

There are many teaching and learning benefits from history labs. Students practice doing history for the purpose of making historically informed arguments, and instructors can use this memorable hands-on work to reinforce content knowledge and make connections to new material. Instructors can also help their students prepare for a more extensive research project by using history labs to scaffold further learning.

SAMPLE HISTORY LAB ASSIGNMENT

Maya Civilization History Lab

1. Divide up the following group roles (In case of three, divide up the Researcher's role among the group.):
   a. *Leader*: Keeps the group on task, makes sure all of the questions are fully answered, assists with research, asks the instructor questions.
   b. *Writer*: Takes the lead on writing the answers and directs the other group members on how to contribute to the written answers, assists with research.
   c. *Contextualizer*: Makes sure answers are based on historical context and that context is incorporated into the answers, assists with research.
   d. *Researcher*: Directs the group in sifting through sources and deciding which items to focus on, makes connections among artifacts.
2. Note on your shared document how you divided the roles.

Introduction: As you read in the textbook selection, the Maya was a flourishing civilization in Central America that preceded the Aztecs. Europeans did not encounter the Maya at the height of their civilization, but there were still remnants of Maya life and ancestry throughout Central America. Studying the Maya more closely allows us to understand that the Europeans did not encounter primitive, stone-age people but rather highly developed, agriculturally based civilizations.

Step 1: Full Group (8 minutes). Look through the background information on the Maya found here: https://www.ancient.eu/Maya_Civilization/. Note that the article discusses the chronology of the Maya, dividing them into different periods (see the dates). The *Context* person should keep the website open and find the relevant dates for the artifacts (see next step).

Step 2: Full Group (10 minutes). Look through this digital archive of Maya artifacts from the Smithsonian Institution: http://tinyurl.com/bdhydppx. *Contextualizer*: Notice the dates and compare the dates to the periods listed on the Maya Civilization website from step 1.

Questions:

1. Investigate the Sources (15 minutes). Working together, choose five or six different artifacts, read the information about each one, and look at the larger images, clicking through the pictures if there is more than one. *Investigation Question: From your overall look at five or six artifacts and the provided context, what can you learn about life in the Maya civilization during this time period? (five sentences minimum).* Resist making broad generalizations (example: "All Maya people were religious."); instead, try to answer narrowly and specifically. What did they seem to value? Were these objects only functional, or did they serve other purposes? What sort of person might use or make these objects? Where were the objects made? and so on. Discuss the five or six objects as a general group, not each object in depth.
2. Make an Argument (15 minutes). Choose one artifact out of the five or six you looked at, and paste a picture of it in your answer. *Based on this object and the secondary source historical context, to what extent were the Maya a complex society?* Answer the question with an argument and discuss the significance of your object in depth. Connect the object to the relevant historical context. Use these questions to guide your thinking: What aspects of Maya society does this object help us understand? Why? How does this object connect to other aspects of Maya society?

NOTES

1. Nancy Shoemaker, "Where Is the History Lab Course?," *Perspectives on History*, January 1, 2009, https://www.historians.org/publications-and-directories/perspectives-on-history/january-2009/where-is-the-history-lab-course.

2. ShawnaKim Lowey-Ball, "History by Text and Thing," *Perspectives on History*, February 26, 2020, https://www.historians.org/publications-and-directories/perspectives-on-history/march-2020/history-by-text-and-thing.

3. Joel M. Sipress and David J. Voelker, "From Learning History to Doing History: Beyond the Coverage Model," in *Exploring Signature Pedagogies: Approaches to Teaching Disciplinary Habits of Mind*, ed. Regan A. R. Gurung, Nancy L. Chick, and Aeron Haynie (Sterling, VA: Stylus Publishing, 2009), 26.

4. Christine Baron, "Structuring Historic Site-Based History Laboratories for Teacher Education," *The Journal of Museum Education* 39, no. 1 (2014): 12.

5. Carla Vecchiola, "Digging in the Digital Archives: Engaging Students in an Online American History Survey," *The History Teacher* 53, no. 1 (November 2019): 107.

6. Vecchiola, "Digging in the Digital Archives," 111–12.

7. The relevant archives are Jamestown Rediscovery, "Explore the Artifacts," accessed September 9, 2023, https://historicjamestowne.org/collections/artifacts/; Tom Costa, "The Geography of Slavery in Virginia," accessed September 9, 2023, http://www2.vcdh.virginia.edu/gos/; Center for Digital Research in the Humanities, "Journals of the Lewis & Clark Expedition," accessed September 9, 2023, https://lewisandclarkjournals.unl.edu/; Boston Public Library, "The Liberator (Boston, Mass.: 1831–1865)," accessed September 9, 2023, https://www.digitalcommonwealth.org/collections/commonwealth:9w032b61n.

8. Lisa M. Lane, "Constructing the Past Online: Discussion Board as History Lab," *The History Teacher* 47, no. 2 (February 2014): 197–207. Lane advocates for students finding documents themselves through internet searching. While finding sources is a useful skill and might be the focus of a lesson, for this type of history lab assignment, the goal is to mimic the experience of archival research.

9. Furman University Department of History, "Succession Era Newspaper Editorials," accessed September 9, 2023, https://scholarexchange.furman.edu/secession-editorials/.

10. Center for Digital Research in the Humanities, "Journals of the Lewis & Clark Expedition," accessed September 9, 2023, https://lewisandclarkjournals.unl.edu/.

11. The benefits of peer instruction have been well-documented, particularly in Ken Bain, *Super Courses: The Future of Teaching and Learning* (Princeton: Princeton University Press, 2021). See especially chapter 8, "Peer Instruction and Then Some."

12. David W. Johnson and Roger T. Johnson, "An Overview of Cooperative Learning," Cooperative Learning Institute, accessed September 7, 2022, http://www.co-operation.org/what-is-cooperative-learning.

13. Alison Burke, "Group Work: How to Use Groups Effectively," *The Journal of Effective Teaching* 11, no. 2 (2011): 88.

14. Vecchiola, "Digging in the Digital Archives," 111.

15. "Search results for: Mayas, 1000s, 1550s, Images, Mayas, page 1," Smithsonian Institution," Collections Search Center, accessed September 15, 2022, https://collections.si.edu/search/results.htm?q=Mayas&fq=online_media_type%3A%22Images%22&fq=culture%3A%22Mayas%22&view=grid&date.slider=1000s%2C1550s.

16. Vecchiola, "Digging in the Digital Archives," 5. The format for the "Investigate" questions derives directly from some of the prompts Carla Vecchiola provides in her article.

17. Jay C. Percell, "Lessons from Alternative Grading: Essential Qualities of Teacher Feedback," *Clearing House* 90, no. 4 (2017): 111–15.

18. Bain, *Super Courses*, 137.

19. "Search results for: Mayas, 1500s, 1550s, Images, Mayas, page 1," Smithsonian Institution, Collections Search Center, accessed September 15, 2022, https://collections.si.edu/search/results.htm?q=Mayas&fq=online_media_type%3A%22Images%22&fq=culture%3A%22Mayas%22&view=grid&date.slider=1500s%2C1550s.

20. "Whistling Jar," Smithsonian Institution, National Museum of the American Indian, accessed September 15, 2022, https://americanindian.si.edu/collections/search/objects/NMAI_266049?objects%5B0%5D=item_1618110f3a7d.

21. An example of a website that brings together both primary sources and conversations among historians is *Commonplace: The Journal of Early American Life*, accessed June 5, 2023, https://commonplace.online.

22. The SlaveVoyages Consortium, accessed September 22, 2022, https://www.SlaveVoyages.org.

23. Cartography Associates, "David Rumsey Map Collection," accessed September 22, 2022, https://www.davidrumsey.com/home.

24. Lowey-Ball, "History by Text and Thing."

Chapter 3

Board Games for Nongamer Instructors

"Let's play a game." Few phrases will change the atmosphere of a classroom faster. Because students often see playing as the opposite of learning, it feels subversive to play in class. Instructors know, of course, that there are many learning benefits attached to play, but not all instructors feel confident in their ability to teach through play.

Over the past decades, scholarly interest in games and learning in general, and history games in particular, has increased. Many instructors enjoy games personally and want to bring the benefits of gaming into the classroom and to connect with students who might also be gamers. What if, however, the instructor is not a gamer or board game enthusiast?[1] Is the barrier to entry too high to use games in the classroom? This chapter explores the use of tabletop games in the classroom for nongamer instructors. It will overview the literature on games and learning, provide practical suggestions for non-gamers to use games in the classroom, and elicit further thinking about customizing the approach to each instructor and classroom.

IN THEORY

The scholarly literature on games and learning is extensive.[2] The more particular discussion about games and history education is similarly vast.[3] Scholars agree that games do some things particularly well. Many scholars point out that normal content delivery methods such as lecture or reading are weak on helping students apply their knowledge. Games, by contrast, force players to put their "knowledge into action," which then leads them to transfer "action into knowledge."[4]

Well-crafted games provide a symbiotic experience of (1) gaining knowledge, (2) making choices, (3) learning from those choices, and (4) adjusting the strategy as new knowledge is obtained. That sequence of complex decision-making is difficult to replicate in a lecture class. Many scholars also note that games motivate students to engage in learning and take control of their learning. Games are also adaptable to a variety of contexts and learning goals and incorporate opportunities for low-stakes failure and mistakes, which can lead to deeper learning, especially if the instructor guides students through the experience.[5]

Much of the discussion about the use of games to achieve learning goals centers on the benefits of play. It is not simply about fun—though that is part of it. Scholars note that creating or using an environment centered on play (i.e., a game) gives participants the freedom to "experiment with new identities, safely explore choices and consequences, and push the boundaries of a system."[6] Play can lead to creativity, problem-solving, and seeing events or ideas from a new perspective. Play also creates opportunities for "non-linear experiential learning" as players explore the world of the game and its limits and opportunities.

No scholars go so far as to argue that games solve all learning problems or are effective in every context.[7] Rather, scholars agree that instructors must use games as one of many tools to achieve learning goals. In that context, there is no inherent benefit to being a game enthusiast in order to use games effectively. Any instructor who is committed to providing unique and effective learning experiences for students to achieve learning goals can use games as one strategy among many. The instructor's commitment to the learning goals will determine the effectiveness of the game as a learning experience.

While there are many benefits to using games to enhance and encourage student learning, do those benefits, or others, translate to learning history in particular? Perhaps controversially, scholars of games and history hone in on one particular feature of games that makes them particularly well-suited to exploring and evaluating history. Through games, Tracy Worthington notes, "students begin to realize history is not a pure science: history is personal, messy, and because of the impossible size and scope of the human experience, both selective and representational."[8]

Several scholars have unpacked Worthington's ideas and expanded on them. Scholars of games and history find many parallels between games (both tabletop and video) and films in their portrayals of history. They note that both game designers and filmmakers have to make particular choices to make their depiction of events playable or watchable. While those choices might lead to sacrifices in historical accuracy in some areas, games and films both "do the work of history, the curated representation of the past to those in the present."[9] The choices that game designers make are different from the choices that academic historians (i.e., those presenting their findings via text) make, but scholars are quick to point out that all historians present a version of the past.[10]

Jeremiah McCall introduces the concept of games as "historical problem spaces," which historians and students can analyze by examining the "core components" of games and—most potent—why game designers made the choices they did in presenting the game and the history. In that way, game designers function as public historians, and their work can be compared to traditional historiography in terms of the choices all historians make in interpreting the historical record.

In some ways, as McCall notes, games are a particularly inviting entry point for instructors to introduce the concept of how historians interpret and present the past, because games exist within a set of clearly defined parameters. That is, the games must work out mathematically, so the options for how game designers present the past are necessarily curtailed. The limits of the medium simplify the presentation options, making it easier for beginner students to think about the work of historical interpretation. Because game design presents to learners a discourse or a system for critical evaluation, the potential for teaching historical thinking through games, especially to novice historians, is particularly potent.[11]

Further, it is the playability of games that gives them their unique place in the construction of history. Because students are playing games—and are fully aware that it is a game—they are less likely to accept a game's presentation of the past as wholly accurate. To take an example from one of the original modern educational games, very few students playing *The Oregon Trail*, set in the 1840s' American West, will believe that hunting simply involved positioning a gun to shoot a bear or deer instead of a few pixelated trees. They will, however, understand that traveling westward meant managing food supplies. Further, they will have felt the anxiety that comes from seeing food supplies dwindle and sicknesses increase.

That engagement primes them for deeper comprehension of both the sources and how historians construct narratives of the past. While a student might not unpack all the layers of choices that are intrinsic to constructing the past (whether in a game or on a page), instructors can direct attention and discussion to the scholarly debate behind the game.[12] The engagement that a game provides has a big payoff in deeper development of historical thinking skills.

For another example, the rule book for the game *Founding Fathers*, designed by Christian Leonhard and Jason Matthews, clearly states the goal of the game: "Your goal in Founding Fathers is to emerge from the Philadelphia Convention acknowledged by all as the true Father of the Constitution due to your outstanding contributions to the final document."[13] Instructors can take this stated goal and lead students through either a cursory or in-depth study of the historiography to examine other major arguments in the field and how this game's argument fits in. Once students have played the game and worked to try to achieve the stated goal, the instructor can capitalize on the provided setup for a robust discussion about the founding fathers, their real-life goals, and the current debates among historians.

Academic historians still might quibble that the game is an unnecessary step in the learning process. Why not simply have a discussion of founding fathers' historiography? Isn't the game a needless waste of time? The answer is found in an examination of the audience. While graduate history students might not need extrinsic motivation to discuss scholarly debates, an eleventh grader or a university sophomore music major taking a general education history class might benefit significantly from the welcoming environment of a game. Those students might find themselves talking and thinking about a topic in which they are not otherwise interested.

Monopoly is perhaps the perfect example, as many more people have played *Monopoly* than read an academic treatise on monopolies. In addition, the people playing *Monopoly* probably do not have much interest in monopolies as a subject of historical analysis, but they have still spent hours of their lives playing a game on the topic.[14] The same could be said for any number of films. Professional historians ignore and belittle nonacademic forms of history at their peril, but more important, they can engage with them to the benefit of all.

There is another aspect of games that instructors should take seriously, particularly considering the decline of the history major in general.[15] Phillip Payne demonstrates how games and game design in the classroom can be used to teach public history. He challenges students to design history games and then to use the experience to articulate the marketable skills they have gained from transforming historical content into a game. Payne argues that analyzing games draws students out of their comfort zone and helps them think about history in new ways—both in terms of the historical content and how it is presented to and consumed by the public.[16]

Choosing Games

When considering games for classroom use, there are a number of potential pitfalls that instructors must consider. First, as game designers translate historical content into games, they may make controversial choices regarding representation. Gabriel McKee and Daniela Wolin discuss games based on ancient history and archaeology in particular and note "some elements will always need to be simplified, essentialized, or left out. These retellings and storylines can come at a cost, as certain narratives and storylines can be perpetuated by games, detrimentally reinforcing past and present stereotypes."[17]

Historian Patrick Rael acknowledges the issue of whose history is represented in a game and uses it to spark discussion about representation and the dialogue between the present and the past. He leads his students through comparisons of board games that portray issues such as slavery in different ways, and in so doing, he uses a potential pitfall of games to guide his students to deeper critical thinking about how historians and game designers portray historical events.[18]

Another potential problem with using games to explore history is the presence of counterfactuals. Unless the game is a carefully designed reenactment, there will be some element of counterfactuals in games, either through simplification or by allowing a variety of outcomes that did not happen historically.[19] Although this can be a problem if an instructor is trying to use a game to teach a narrative about the past, many game scholars argue that counterfactuals open up useful discussions. For instance, in *Founding Fathers*, students might end up creating a Constitution that includes popular election of presidents, instead of the electoral college system. This option creates an opportunity to discuss the pros and cons of both ideas.

As the instructor leads students through the debriefing discussion, the class can compare the game outcome with the real historical record and think about the reasons for the differences. This discussion has the possibility for deep historical thinking that might not be as rich if the students had not lived the counterfactual outcomes through gameplay.[20]

Nevertheless, some games are better than others for classroom use. Scholars note that the best games balance three aspects: "pedagogical elements, simulation elements and game elements."[21] If these elements are out of balance, it may be more difficult to achieve the desired learning outcomes. A game that leans too far toward a simulation risks being too complex for classroom use. On the other hand, a game might be fun but without any substantive connection to the content or without directing meaningful learning. This might be especially true for trivia-based games, which may have a place in test review but do not provide an immersive simulation of a historical event. Instructors need to test out different types of games and consider modifying existing games to make them effective classroom tools.[22]

Proponents of historical video games for classroom use argue that these games are beneficial because they allow players to experience the simulated historical environment. In addition, some historical games—and video games in particular—emphasize the unfolding of history as a process. This can be seen, once again, in the example of *The Oregon Trail*, where part of the creators' goal was to simulate the experience of traveling west. A significant part of the game play involves the player waiting for time to pass or the wagon to move along the simulated trail.[23] Savvy instructors can take advantage of the simulated historical environment to direct student learning and reflection.

The research shows that games can be an effective tool to stimulate deep learning; however, the instructor must build the bridge between the game and the learning goals. Whether in the game selection process or in modifying a game, creating lessons to scaffold the game, or crafting the debrief session, the instructor's role is critical to ensure that the full potential of games for learning is realized. It should be evident, then, that a teacher looking to use games does not need to be a board game enthusiast or a gamer in their personal life. Instead, the instructor needs to prioritize student learning and consider how games can help achieve learning goals.

IN PRACTICE

While it may be easy to agree with the theoretical benefits of games in the classroom, nongamer instructors may still face some challenges when trying to use games effectively. There is no question that board game enthusiasts will have an advantage when it comes to selecting games because their knowledge of game types and specific games may be extensive. In addition, gamers will have to do less work in teaching students how to play games; they may intuitively understand how a game works, or they may have played the game before, or they are happy to spend their personal time testing out games for classroom use.

Lacking this advantage should not necessarily discourage the nongamer instructor. This section will explore several practical steps instructors can take to select games and use them effectively. The first and most important component to remember is that the learning goal is the primary consideration. Before developing game-based lessons, the instructor should take time to think about what he wants students to be able to do when the lesson is complete and how that result contributes to the overall learning goals of the course.

Planning Game-Based Lessons

Learning goals might range from cooperative learning to reviewing specific content to comparing presentations of history or many other ideas. Consider how students will demonstrate their achievement of the goal. Will they write a reflection, make a game review video, create their own board game, write a historiographical essay, answer multiple-choice questions, or something else? How will their achievement of the goal help them succeed in one of the course's summative assessments?

Next, in crafting game-based lessons, it is tempting to spend the most time on the game itself. Research shows, however, that the most learning-focused way to use games is to focus on the debrief session after the game. Students need enough initial context to understand the content of the game, and then they should play it at least twice. Following the game, the class can reflect on learning, connections, and remaining questions in the debrief session (which is discussed thoroughly below).

Alternatively, the game can be played initially to spark interest in the subject, then the class can thoroughly explore the content. The game is then played again, followed by a debrief session. With that approach the instructor must consider how much time she is devoting to the game. If the game takes several class periods to play, the instructor needs to justify it by including a comparable number of context and debriefing sessions. A short or simple game might be sufficient to reap the benefits of games, if deployed effectively.

Depending on the learning goals, the historical content sessions might simply provide the historical background to the game, perhaps with a special focus on the characters or groups who are featured in the game. With this approach, however, the game risks being an afterthought—something fun but ultimately unnecessary to achieving the learning goals. A more integrated approach carefully considers the game's unique contribution to the learning experience and uses the context sessions to thoroughly prepare students to learn from the game.

Many historical board games function as a gamified simulation of a historical event. Toward that end, therefore, instructors can prepare students to play a game in the same way that they would prepare students for an in-class debate or any other type of in-class simulation. If there are characters or factions in the game, class time should be devoted to understanding them, through reading primary sources and, perhaps, familiarizing students with the main historiographical interpretations of the individuals involved.

Whatever historical scenario the game is simulating should be equally well-explored by immersing students in the "world of the game." This exploration might be complimented by homework assignments that require students to watch videos, listen to podcasts, and read primary and secondary sources that build up their factual knowledge of the time period and event. Students can answer questions or write essays to establish the historical context of the game. Instructors can also lead the class in a discussion of whether the game's particular focus is the best way to understand the historical time period or idea. What are the benefits of examining the event featured in the game? What event might be better?

For example, *Freedom: The Underground Railroad* by Brian Mayer focuses on the interconnections between the abolitionist movement and the underground railroad in the United States in the decades leading up to the Civil War. While, the Civil War itself is the subject of many board games and wargames, *Freedom* focuses instead on the ideologies that were tearing the nation apart. Class context sessions could include discussions about the pros and cons of *Freedom* in contrast to a game such as *American Civil War* by Chris Perello that focuses on strategies and tactics.[24]

It is also necessary to prepare the students to take on the historical roles of the game. Are students taking on a real persona or are they functioning as a third-party force who manipulates historical characters? What specific historical or in-game contingencies will they need to consider, and how do those contingencies relate to the accepted narrative? As a lead-up to the game, students might write an essay or answer questions from the perspective of a character in the game.

Finally, how does understanding the "world of the game" relate to the learning goals and the formative and summative assessments? For a game to be worth the use of class time, it must contribute substantially toward the learning goals. As the instructor immerses students in the historical content and prepares them to simulate an event, he must give attention to the final outcome. If students will complete the experience by taking a multiple-choice test, a portion of the questions must draw from knowledge or experience gained from playing the game. If students will create their own game for the summative assessment, instructors must build in time to discuss how game designers make choices and how game mechanics help to simulate the real-world events.

As an example, the game *Operation F.A.U.S.T.* by Robert Burke provides a solid foundation upon which to plan a game-based lesson.[25] The game simulates art dealers' and patrons' attempts to recover art that the Nazis looted during World War II. The game provides an immersive experience that is not simply a skin on another game; it is packed with historical information and provides a simulation of the emotional experience of using deception to recover the stolen art.

Such an effective game provides an opportunity to explore a part of World War II that often does not warrant much attention in history textbooks. In fact, students may need to be told that the game is based on real events and people. If used correctly, the game can open opportunities to explore the lives and contributions of the major participants, lead to in-depth discussions about civilian participation in war, and provide an entry point to examine the role of art in defining culture.

Operation F.A.U.S.T. is a good example not only of the potential of games but also how instructors can miss that opportunity if they are not intentional about using games within a larger course design. Because games are fun, it is tempting to simply unleash them on the class without careful setup and debriefing. That approach not only wastes valuable class time playing an uncontextualized game but also misses the true benefit that games bring to history classrooms. That is, games provide an emotional, experiential simulation of a historical event, which can either be entertainment-focused and shallow or immersive, memorable, and profound.

The potential of games is also why the debrief session after the game is critical for achieving learning goals.[26] The importance of the debrief is another reason why it is not necessary to be a board game expert to use games effectively. An instructor who has a clear understanding of (1) the learning goal(s), (2) the experience of playing the game, and (3) the pros and cons of the game as a learning experience can facilitate an effective debrief session. If games are used semi-regularly throughout the term, it is helpful to consistently use the same set of questions as a starting point for the discussion.

Effective debrief questions recognize the emotional, social, and cognitive aspects of playing a game and address all of them. Questions might include the following:

1. What did you like or not like about the game?
2. How did you feel while playing the game?
3. What key choices did you make that affected the outcome of the game?
4. What connections do you see between the historical content and the game? What connections are missing?
5. How do the rules of the game compare to real-world limitations and contingencies?
6. How did the game allow for counterfactual thinking, and how does that experience deepen your understanding of the real events?
7. How could you modify the game to make it more effective in either the presentation of history or the simulation of the historical events?

Because games are a fun, communal activity, it is very tempting to skip the debrief or rush through it during the last five minutes of class. Giving in to that temptation risks not taking full advantage of what games offer. The debrief is an important time for students to think critically about their experience and connect it to the pregame learning. The instructor might choose to end class with just a few of the more emotional or experiential questions and then lead students through a deeper discussion during the following class. Or the instructor can create a reflection assignment in which students respond to one or more of the debrief questions, perhaps through an online class discussion board so students can benefit from each other's perspectives.

Using Games

Some instructors might be intrigued by the idea of using games but feel intimidated about learning games well enough themselves to facilitate them in class. Similarly, some instructors might be interested in the learning benefits of games but are not board game enthusiasts or any type of gamer. There are several ways to overcome these challenges.

First, inviting a board game enthusiast to visit the class and help run the game can be an effective solution. Given the rising popularity of board games, a school or university library may have a gamer on staff, or the librarians can assist in finding someone. The outside expert needs to have played the game recently and be familiar with the finer points of the rules. They might teach the instructor the game before the class session so that the instructor is somewhat familiar with the game and can answer some of the students' questions. Having a game expert in the classroom is critical to ensuring that students start playing the game quickly and accurately.

Another option is to start with simpler or more familiar games and work up to more complex games, perhaps over the course of several offerings of the class. A simple game can be just as effective as a more complex game if it is used correctly by the instructor. To use *Monopoly* as an example again, most students are familiar with the game and could begin playing with minimal instruction time, but teachers could use it to deepen and enrich discussions of twentieth-century capitalism. The history of the game and its relationship to scholarly debates about society and economics provide rich fodder for discussion, despite the simplicity of the game itself.

There are other alternatives for the instructor who does not want to take on the responsibility of being the game expert. Almost every board game has "how to play" videos freely available on the internet. While it may be useful for the instructor to watch these, it is even better to assign videos and the rule book to students as homework before the game begins. A short quiz that is autograded in a school's learning management system can ensure that students come to class ready to play. There are also "play-through" videos of many board games. These are akin to giving the viewer a seat at the table as a game is played. A play-through video of a complex game may be an hour long or more, so it might only be appropriate for the instructor to use as a preparation resource.

It is important to note, however, that reading and watching the instructions often is not enough to get a game started quickly and keep it going smoothly. There is no substitute for having an expert in the room, so another option is to designate a group of students to be the game experts. If the class is playing several games, students can each take a turn as part of the expert team. If only one or two games are used, the instructor might offer extra credit or some other incentive; sometimes the chance to be the expert is incentive enough, especially if the students enjoy games personally. The student experts should play the game several times before class and then spend the class time rotating around the room troubleshooting and answering questions.

There are a few other logistical choices that need consideration before deploying games. First, for all but the simplest games, it is necessary for students to play the game at least twice. The first time is more about the rules and the moves; the second time can focus on strategy and the immersive experience of the game. If an instructor is committed to using a game, he must budget adequate time to play twice. It is also important to note that, while most games include a "suggested playing time," the time for the first game might be much longer than anticipated.

Second, instructors must consider the roles they are asking students to take on as part of the game. Many games might require students to play from a perspective with which they personally disagree. In politics-based simulations, such as *Campaign Manager 2008*, students might be playing a side that goes against their personal politics. In *Memoir '44*, gameplay requires that each player takes a turn playing the Allied side and the Axis side, which provides balance to the game. Some games require bluffing in order to win. The game *Secret Hitler* requires bluffing, and it requires that someone plays the role of Hitler, even though the focus of the game is on consensus-building in politics and how even an unpopular minority faction can win an election.[27]

Because of the emotional potency of games, it is important to consider the class makeup, the maturity level, the familiarity with board gaming as a form of inquiry, and the learning goals when selecting games. A course focused on game design and historiography can use more emotionally and topically complex games than an introductory survey course can. In both instances, the instructor must spend time discussing the choices game designers make and how games provide an opportunity for critical evaluation. The instructor must be fully aware that games carry more social and emotional weight than a textbook reading. The excuse of "it's just a game" will not be a sufficient reply to students who react negatively to a game that the instructor has not properly prepared them to play.[28]

To best optimize the use of games, instructors should consider how games can deepen learning in a single-topic unit. World War II is an easy example since the games available range from battle simulations (*Memoir '44*) to cultural explorations (*Operation F.A.U.S.T.*) to political conflict (*Churchill*) and many others.[29] As students play more games, they can compare them to each other, and by the end of the unit, students have a shared set of experiences that they can discuss and connect to the accepted narrative. While an instructor cannot fully recreate a historical event, board games provide a unique opportunity to experience a simulated version of an event, and the more games are used, the more angles on the event students can experience.

If an instructor cannot devote a whole unit to board games, another approach is to use several games over the course of the semester, perhaps by linking the games to one theme. The benefit of using several games is that students become more adept at playing board games and can compare the games to each other. For example, a series of games on a theme such as war or politics can be interwoven into a course and provide a consistent method of inquiry.[30]

Benefiting from Games

There are two ways in which instructors can expand the scope of how they use games in class. One way is to assign students to tell "the story of the game" at the game's conclusion; the other is to employ a game creation assignment. Both can be useful ways to benefit fully from taking class time to play games and can help to achieve learning goals.

As students conclude a game, they should be able to narrate the created history of their simulated event. It may take some nudging from the instructor for students to separate their gameplay from the created event, but it is a useful historical thinking exercise. If the teacher asks students to tell the story of the game, students might be tempted to rehearse the individual moves (e.g., "then I pulled a card and had to move my marker back to the start of the tracker") rather than create a narrative.

Teachers can use a scaffolding assignment to bridge the gap between gameplay and narrative. Ask students to choose three key events that determined the outcome of the game; then ask them to turn those three events into a historical narrative (likely counterfactual), without any gameplay narration. Students can take it a step further by writing the events as a newspaper article or making a video as if they are a news desk anchor. Instructors can close the learning loop by asking students to reflect on choices they made as simulated historical actors and compare their "story of the game" to the accepted narrative. Students can be pushed to consider how creating their story compares to how historians interpret and create narratives of the past.

Once students have played several games themselves, instructors might choose to assign students to create their own game and game book. This is probably best done as a group project due to the amount of work involved, but instructors might give students leeway to take charge of specific parts of the game and receive an individual grade for their contribution. Scholars point to many benefits for students in creating games.[31] Most important, the assignment gives students freedom to develop and pursue their own ideas, from the topic of the game down to the intricacies of game design. In addition, students have the opportunity to express their creativity, whether it be in how the game looks or in the complexity of gameplay.

In drafting the assignment instructions, teachers should be aware that board games are difficult to create. In particular, if students have played several games in class, they might have some idea of the complexity that is possible.

The instructor might want to put some limits in place so that students end up with games that are playable. Second, the instructor should consider if she wants to allow students to simply create a new skin for an existing game (for example, *World War II Monopoly*) or to what degree students can borrow ideas from existing games.

In addition, just like in a traditional research process, a narrow focus is more feasible for students than a broad survey. Students might propose a game about the entire U.S. Civil War, but the instructor might guide them to narrow their focus to just "nursing during the Civil War" or "international politics and the Civil War." A single event or idea will allow students to do more in-depth research and will be easier to translate onto the game board.

Instructors also must consider to what degree they will allow counterfactuals. Although all games use counterfactuals, allowing wildly ahistorical outcomes might circumvent some of the learning goals. One way to rein in the use of counterfactuals is to require that students explain their game design choices in the game book.

Finally, if instructors plan to use a game design assignment, they need to build in discussions of game design throughout the course. The instructor does not need to be a game designer in order to have effective discussions, although bringing in a game designer to visit the class would enhance the project considerably. In the same way that historians make choices about how to present history, game designers make choices about how to portray an event. Pulling back the curtain on that decision-making process and challenging students to do it themselves opens up useful conversations about how historians craft history.[32]

CUSTOMIZE

Instructors should customize their use of games according to their interests and comfort level with facilitating games. One instructor might feel motivated to thoroughly learn a game and enjoy the opportunity to guide students through gameplay. Another might never feel confident about their ability to answer rules-related questions. In addition to the suggestions regarding bringing in outside expertise discussed above, there are several ways in which instructors can personalize their use of games so that both instructor and student succeed.

One option is to assign students to review a board game in the same way that they might review a film or a historical monograph, particularly as part of more extensive class discussions about the various ways history is presented. Whether students present their review to the full class or a group, or complete a written assignment, this is a way to use games without using class time for game play. Similarly, the instructor might use board game review videos as examples, rather than playing a game in class.

Classes with a focus on public history can produce and present board game reviews to a general audience, perhaps working with a local library that holds a board game collection. Along the same lines, classes could create forward-facing presentations on the variety of ways history is presented, with board games included alongside scholarly books and articles, museum exhibits, and films. These types of assignments can support learning goals focused on evaluating the work that historians do.

On the other end of the spectrum, some instructors may so enjoy using games that they want to create games specific to their course content. One way to do this is to have students create games on the given topic and then have the class work to improve the best one. The instructor can then build off that prototype to create a game that fits perfectly with the course material. The process might take several years, but it includes several opportunities for student involvement, either through game design or playtesting.

Another approach is to take game components or a complete game and adapt them to simulate a historical event or idea. A basic example of this is the many "skins" that designers have created for *Monopoly*. While the approach is thoroughly explained elsewhere, the guiding idea is to take the conceit of an existing game and adapt it to teach historical context.[33] For example, Reuben Klamer's *The Game of Life*, when stripped down to its basic elements, is a simulation of life from early adulthood to retirement. Instructors can use the basic template to explore the lives of any number of historical characters, from the common people of Renaissance Rome to early modern explorers to industrial labor union activists.

Adapting the action elements—whether game cards, board spaces, or the like—from their generic forms (having babies, buying a house, etc.) to historically specific events (joining a labor strike, finding adequate medical care, etc.) allows students to explore the lives of many types of people, and instructors can customize the content to the exact needs of their courses. Similarly, a game that simulates a life, journey, or choice can be customized to reflect a different historical context. For example, an instructor could adapt the card game version of *The Oregon Trail* to instead simulate journeys along the ancient Silk Road.

CONCLUSION

There are many benefits to using games to teach history. Students can actively play through interpretations of history and consider how the complexity of history relates to its presentation. Instructors who want to use games must focus first on the learning goals and then determine their comfort level with using games in the classroom. This chapter discussed how teachers can use games to introduce and reinforce how historians craft narratives and argue about interpretations. As students experience game designers' choices through gameplay, they recognize how historians interpret and present historical arguments and compare those representations to other presentations of history.

At the same time, instructors must choose games carefully by considering learning outcomes when selecting games. Games may have content issues related to representation and counterfactuals that the instructor must recognize and decide how to approach for effective learning. In addition, instructors should look for games that balance learning, simulation, and fun in order to help students benefit fully from games.

It is not necessary for instructors to be board game enthusiasts to use games effectively. As long as the learning goals are the central focus, the instructor can use games in a variety of ways that align with their comfort level and resources. Because of the centrality of the learning goals, the instructor must plan lessons that adequately contextualize the game and then fully debrief the experience of playing the game.

To complete the learning loop, instructors can build on the foundation of playing games in class by challenging students to turn their gameplay into counterfactual historical narratives, which can then provide the basis for further discussion. Another option is to have students create their own games and game books, perhaps in place of a traditional research paper. Students might also review board games, either as part of class discussion or as a way to engage the public in historical thinking.

Above all, instructors should find the approach that works best for them and their students. While instructors might be intimidated by using complex board games in class if they are not tabletop gamers themselves, there are many ways for instructors to feel confident that they are using games effectively to achieve learning goals and increase opportunities for experiential learning.

NOTES

1. While the term *gamer* is most often applied to people who play video or computer games, with the recent resurgence of tabletop games (board games), strategy games, and the like, gamer also applies to game hobbyists in a more general sense.

2. An attempt to catalog the full discussion would be a significant undertaking. Here are some places to start: Jan L. Plass, Richard E. Mayer, and Bruce D. Homer, eds., *Handbook of Game-Based Learning* (Cambridge, MA: MIT Press, 2020); Karen

Schrier, *Learning, Education & Games*, 3 vols. (Pittsburgh: Carnegie Mellon University, 2014–2019).

3. Some ways to start exploring this literature include the following: Jeremiah McCall, "Bibliography," Gaming the Past, https://gamingthepast.net/theory-practice/bibliography/; Liz Davidson, *Beyond Solitaire* (podcast audio), accessed June 30, 2023, https://beyondsolitaire.buzzsprout.com/; Patrick Rael, "Bibliography of Work on Game Studies and History," *Ludica* (blog), October 3, 2021, https://boardgamegeek.com/blogpost/123281/bibliography-work-game-studies-and-history; Society for History Education, Inc., "*The History Teacher*: Gaming in the History Classroom," accessed June 28, 2023, https://www.societyforhistoryeducation.org/games.html.

4. David Crookall and Warren Thorngate, eds., "Acting, Knowing, Learning, Simulating, Gaming," Simulation and Gaming 40, no. 1 (2009): 8–9, 16.

5. Lisa Galarneau, "Authentic Learning Experiences through Play: Games, Simulations and the Construction of Knowledge," *Proceedings of DiGRA 2005 Conference: Changing Views—Worlds in Play*, vol. 3, Digital Games Research Association (2005); Lauren Hays and Mark Hayse, "Game On! Experiential Learning with Tabletop Games," in *The Experiential Library: Transforming Academic and Research Libraries through the Power of Experiential Learning*, ed. Pete McDonnell (New York: Chandos, 2017); Brian Mayer and Christopher Harris, *Libraries Got Game: Aligned Learning through Modern Board Games* (Chicago: ALA Editions, 2010), 5–6; Jan L. Plass, Bruce D. Homer, and Charles K. Kinzer, "Foundations of Game-Based Learning," Educational Psychologist 50, no. 4 (2015): 278.

6. Karen Schrier, *Learning, Education & Games*, vol. 1 (Pittsburgh: Carnegie Mellon University, 2014), 1.

7. Schrier, *Learning, Education & Games*, 1.

8. Tracy Anne Worthington, "Letting Students Control Their Own Learning: Using Games, Role-Plays, and Simulations in Middle School U.S. History Classrooms," *The Social Studies* 109, no. 2 (May 2018): 139.

9. Jeremiah McCall, "The Historical Problem Space Framework: Games as a Historical Medium," *Game Studies* 20, no. 3 (September 2020), http://gamestudies.org/2003/articles/mccall.

10. McCall, "The Historical Problem Space Framework."

11. Jason Begy, "Board Games and the Construction of Cultural Memory," *Games and Culture* 12, nos. 7–8 (2017); Adam Chapman, "Privileging Form Over Content: Analysing Historical Videogames," *Journal of Digital Humanities* 1, no. 2 (2012); Jeremiah McCall, "Navigating the Problem Space: The Medium of Simulation Games in the Teaching of History," *The History Teacher* 46, no. 1 (November 2012): 13–19; Patrick Rael, "Playing with the Past: Teaching Slavery with Board Games," *Perspectives on History: The Newsmagazine of the American Historical Association*, October 13, 2021, https://www.historians.org/research-and-publications/perspectives-on-history/november-2021/playing-with-the-past-teaching-slavery-with-board-games.

12. Matthew Wilhelm Kapell and Andrew B. R. Elliott, eds., *Playing with the Past: Digital Games and the Simulation of History* (New York: Bloomsbury Academic, 2013), 13–14.

13. Christian Leonhard and Jason Matthews, "Founding Fathers: Planner's Guide to the Constitutional Convention" (Sigel, IL: Jolly Roger Games, 2010), 3.

14. Charles Darrow and Elizabeth J. Magie, Monopoly (Pawtucket, RI: Hasbro, 1935), board game.

15. Robert B. Townsend, "Has the Decline in History Majors Hit Bottom?" *Perspectives on History: The Newsmagazine of the American Historical Association*, February 23, 2021, https://www.historians.org/research-and-publications/perspectives-on-history/march-2021/has-the-decline-in-history-majors-hit-bottom-data-from-2018%E2%80%9319-show-lowest-number-since-1980.

16. Phillip Payne, "Skill Building through Game Building in a Public History Class," *Process: A Blog for American History,* May 12, 2016, http://www.processhistory.org/game-building/.

17. Gabriel McKee and Daniela Wolin, "Re-Rolling the Past: Representations and Reinterpretations of Antiquity in Analog and Digital Games: Introduction," *ISAW Papers* 22 (July 21, 2022), https://archive.nyu.edu/bitstream/2451/63888/3/Re-Rolling%20the%20Past%20PDF.pdf.

18. Rael, "Playing with the Past."

19. For some discussion of counterfactuals see Tom Apperley, "Modding the Historians' Code: Historical Verisimilitude and the Counterfactual Imagination," in *Playing with the Past: Digital Games and the Simulation of History*, ed. Matthew Kappell and Andrew Elliot (New York: Bloomsbury Academic, 2013), chap. 12.

20. Derek Bruff, interview with Patrick Rael, *Leading Lines Podcast* (podcast audio), April 18, 2022, https://ir.vanderbilt.edu/handle/1803/17559; Kappell and Elliot, *Playing with the Past*, 7.

21. Galarneau, "Authentic Learning Experiences," 4.

22. Galarneau, "Authentic Learning Experiences," 4.

23. Matt Jancer, "How You Wound Up Playing 'The Oregon Trail' in Computer Class," *Smithsonian Magazine*, July 22, 2016, https://www.smithsonianmag.com/innovation/how-you-wound-playing-em-oregon-trailem-computer-class-180959851/.

24. Brian Mayer, Freedom: The Underground Railroad (Freemont, OH: Academy Games, 2023), board game; Chris Perello, American Civil War (Bakersfield, CA: Decision Games, 2018), board game.

25. Robert Burke, Operation F.A.U.S.T. (Robert Burke Games, 2015), board game.

26. Dave Eng, "Debriefing Games-Based Learning," *UniversityXP* (blog), February 1, 2022, https://www.universityxp.com/blog/2022/2/1/debriefing-games-based-learning; Mark Hayse, "Tabletop Games and 21st Century Skill Practice in the Undergraduate Classroom," *Teaching Theology & Religion* 21, no. 4 (October 2018): 290–1; Scott Nicholson, "Completing the Experience: Debriefing in Experiential and Educational Games," *Journal on Systemics, Cybernetics and Informatics* 11 (2012): 27–31.

27. Richard Borg, Memoir '44 (Los Altos, CA: Days of Wonder, 2004), board game; Mike Boxleiter, Christian Leonhard and Jason Matthews, Campaign Manager 2008 (Roseville, MN: Z-Man Games, 2009), board game; Tommy Maranges, and Max Temkin, Secret Hitler (Chicago: Goat Wolf & Cabbage, 2016), board game.

28. Rael, "Playing with the Past."

29. Mark Herman, Churchill (Hanford, CA: GMT Games, 2015), board game.

30. By comparison, see Patrick Rael, "Proposal for a History Course Built around Tabletop Games," *Ludica* (blog), April 2, 2017, https://boardgamegeek.com/blogpost/64059/proposal-history-course-built-around-tabletop-game.

31. Aleksandra Ilic Rajkovic, Mirjana Senic Ruzic, and Bojan Ljujic, "Board Games as Educational Media: Creating and Playing Board Games for Acquiring Knowledge of History," *IARTEM* e-journal 11, no. 2 (2019): 17. See also Ashley Heim and Emily Holt, "From Bored Games to Board Games: Student-Driven Game Design in the Virtual Classroom," *Journal of Microbiology & Biology Education* 22, no. 1 (2021). There are also many lesson plans about board game creation online.

32. Instructors can find many game design resources to help students create their games. In particular, the podcast series from University XP is an accessible way to learn about game design and can be assigned as homework. Dave Eng, *Experience Points* (podcast audio), https://www.universityxp.com/podcast.

33. Elizabeth George, "Life Lessons: A Game Takes Students to Renaissance Rome," *Perspectives on History: The Newsmagazine of the American Historical Association*, December 1, 2017, https://www.historians.org/research-and-publications/perspectives-on-history/december-2017/life-lessons-a-game-takes-students-to-renaissance-rome.

Chapter 4

Using Stories

Picture an early career teacher delivering a standard introductory lecture on Classical Greek society. The teacher, feeling the pressure to teach to an upcoming test or feeling obligated to cover a set of textbook points, dutifully creates PowerPoint slides for the relevant facts. Slides for religion, social classes, education, women, and so on line up to receive their sets of bullet points. In class, the teacher reads all the bullet points while the students pay attention only long enough to copy them. The teacher may feel that she has adequately covered the topic; the students were never interested enough to notice what the topic was.[1]

Contrast this scenario with the teacher starting class by declaring, "I'm going to tell you a story." She then tells the story of Neaira (a real woman in ancient Athens), including her background, opportunities, choices, limitations, and her interactions with others, and with large-scale events.[2] Along the way, all of the information from the sad bullet-point lecture is interwoven into the story. But the story does not stop there. The instructor pauses the story at moments where the historical record is contested and leads the students through an evaluation of the evidence; students, in turn, contribute to the telling of the story through their analysis. At the end of the session, students respond to a prompt to summarize the content in their notes.

As the course continues, the class can refer to the ancient Grecian's story as shorthand for all they have learned about Greek society. Students experience history, then, not as a set of facts disconnected from the historical process but as a narrative constructed by historians and shaped by individual and collective choices and contingencies.

Before proceeding, it is important to note that there is a difference between examples and the use of stories explained in this chapter. An example illustrates one point, as in "Harriet Tubman was an escaped slave who helped move people along the Underground Railroad." The story approach, explained below, would tell the full story of Harriet Tubman as a way to discuss the sectional crisis of the 1850s in the United States. The approach, therefore, is to use stories not simply to illustrate but as an intriguing and memorable entry point to the historical record and debates about historical narratives.

Encouraging history teachers to tell stories is hardly a new idea. But for early career teachers who are overwhelmed with the number of lessons that must be planned, putting in the work to create story-based lessons seems like a big ask when premade bullet point slides are readily available online. While finding and crafting stories may be labor-intensive, there are many benefits and ways to ease the preparation burden.

For one, story-based lessons can span multiple days, with the instructor periodically referring back to the story. In addition, story-based lessons do not need to be used every day—they are best used to introduce a unit or to dig into a difficult or dull topic. Above all, stories build classroom community by giving the students and teacher shared narratives that they can refer to throughout the course.

Telling stories should not come at the expense of teaching historical literacy—basic knowledge of names, dates, ideas, and events. Rather, students can develop historical literacy in a more attention-sustaining way, while also exercising some agency as amateur historians. Stories can serve, therefore, as an entry point for a time period, event, or idea, providing communal knowledge that the class can deconstruct as the unit progresses.

Instead of waiting until students have memorized enough facts to do "real history," the approach equips students with both information and skills to become historically literate and apply that informational knowledge immediately to do some basic historical work. Stories help students develop as historical thinkers because they see that historians construct history and derive it from multiple, complex perspectives, which they do not accept without interrogation.

IN THEORY

Narratives are the backbone of history as a discipline, and even the driest textbook employs a narrative structure. Narratives can, however, obscure the work that historians do by presenting history as an uncontested series of facts and examples. The solution is not to abandon narrative but rather to uncover how and why historians construct historical narratives. Some teachers take the valuable approach of leading students through analyses of various historical metanarratives. This approach can be a useful way to frame a whole course as well as provide meaning to document analyses, secondary source reading, and class discussion.[3]

The stories approach outlined in this chapter builds on a historiographical approach that sees history as a "a system of stories, some resolved and some not."[4] While there are strengths and weaknesses to this approach, the instructor can demonstrate to students how historians craft these systems of stories from sources and interweave stories to form narratives, all while continually reinterrogating, problematizing, and reinterpreting primary sources. Using stories is a stepping stone to deeper historiographical work because it illuminates this particular view of the past, which all historians may not share.[5]

To unpack the idea further, Clare Hake and Terry Haydn suggest that critical thinking in history involves having students become aware of how history is constructed and experiencing the concept that "the 'jigsaw' can be put together in different ways, to give different versions of the past."[6] Similarly, Diane Ketelle notes that unpacking stories allows students to see "how narratives are silenced, contested, or accepted and what effects they have."[7] Interrogating stories and critically examining the relationships between sources and stories can foster an equalization of power dynamics.

Furthermore, stories are a useful way of working with students' attention cycles. Stories grab interest and provide contrast to other learning strategies, which can help students maintain their attention.[8] Gabriel McNett and other scholars note that storytelling is a particularly potent tool because "humans have a natural disposition for interpreting our experiences as stories."[9] Nevertheless, McNett cautions that stories about individuals "represent a single data point," and instructors should be cautious about using stories to prove or show "a broader trend or concept."[10] Rather than abandoning stories altogether, history instructors can use the narrow scope of a story to discuss how historians translate individual data points into trends and concepts.

Some academic historians have delved deeply into how to use stories in their scholarly work, experimenting with using narrative styles in presenting their research to bridge the gap between the imaginative work of engaging with the past and the archival work of historians. Fred Anderson and Andrew Cayton note that employing specific stories to build historical narratives can emphasize "the historian's role as an active agent in the construction of history."[11]

David Gerwin and Jack Zevin have capitalized on the use of stories in their two pedagogical guides: *Teaching World History as Mystery* and *Teaching U.S. History as Mystery*. Gerwin and Zevin argue that teaching history as a series of mysteries to be uncovered, interpreted, and debated holds students' attention and allows them to recognize how historians reconstruct (or choose to cover up) the past. Their strategy is very engaging and should be added to all history teachers' toolkits. The approach outlined in this chapter emphasizes less of the mystery aspect but echoes the call to involve students in the process of interpreting the past.[12]

Nevertheless, the story-based approach can be problematic. When the instructor presents a story, students may assume that the story unfolded inevitably, and the instructor's presentation of the people and events fully explores their complexity. Instructors can mitigate this danger by including deconstruction exercises that demonstrate and uncover the historical thinking process. Students will then see that historians can and do construct stories in multiple ways.[13]

IN PRACTICE

Using stories to teach a single lesson or to set up a unit is an approach that teachers can duplicate over and over. There are several main elements that instructors should consider. Using these elements can streamline the process of structuring lessons around stories. The steps include finding stories, telling stories, and interweaving historical document analysis into storytelling.

There are many ways to find useful stories. The first thing that instructors should bear in mind is what makes a story particularly useful for (1) teaching content and (2) showing how historians construct history. To begin with, the stories should be about real events, people, and ideas. While there might be uses for fictional stories (see "Customize" section below), in order to reap the benefits of stories for students' historical and historiographical literacy, instructors should choose stories that are derived from historical records, even if there are many possible interpretations of the facts. Using stories about real history also helps with the content coverage demands that many teachers operate under.

When looking for a story about a topic—for example, the Fertile Crescent or the Age of Exploration or the Opium Wars—instructors should look for a person, place, thing, or event that touches most of the main facts they wish to cover. A biographical approach may be the most straightforward, but depending on the content, a story about a place (for example, a specific river or a temple) might be an intriguing way to show change over time.

Commodity histories are also popular ways to trace and anchor historical events. Following the story of tea, cocoa, porcelain, or bananas can anchor several lessons worth of content. Similarly, animal historians provide new perspectives on events by looking at specific animals—from crabs to horses to mosquitos—and examining their place in the narrative.[14]

Whatever the story's main focus, a good guideline for choosing stories is to select the more specific story over the more general. So, for example, telling the story of the black rat that spread the bubonic plague and then spread diseases to the Americas is a better choice for a story than telling the story of all rats. Similarly, telling the story of women's pants is more useful than the narrative of all women's fashions. The learning advantage of a more specific story is that it is more accessible for students to deconstruct and to identify factors such as change over time and causality.

In addition, the most useful stories will connect to all or most of the main content points. While it is fun to tell an anomalous or bizarre story—and there is certainly a place for outrageous stories that grab attention—in order to be able to use stories as a frequent way of learning history, the stories must help to demonstrate or interrogate the accepted narrative. For example, the story of Aiko Herzig-Yoshinaga, a Japanese American who experienced (and later, exposed) internment in California during World War II, may contribute more to historical literacy than a one-in-a-million story of World War II heroics.[15]

Keeping in mind that students will most likely remember the story more than any other facts helps instructors avoid choosing a story that is obscure or runs too far counter to the accepted narrative. For instance, telling the story of the Donner Party—the doomed pioneers who were stranded and starving in the California mountains—as the way to discuss Westward Expansion in the United States might not help very much in reaching content coverage goals. If students leave the lesson thinking that Westward Expansion was all about cannibalism, they might not have the proper context to understand the more mundane aspects that are more common across the historical record. That is not to state categorically that wild stories cannot be used, just that the teacher should keep his content goals as top priority.

The instructor should also choose stories that give opportunities for analyzing the historical record. The most useful stories will be directly derived from primary sources. So, for example, letters and poems written by a Puritan woman not only provides the foundation for a biographical narrative of the woman's life but also gives students an opportunity to examine the sources themselves. The sources are available and accessible to a novice historian and easily connect to the story. By contrast, a story that is cobbled together from brief mentions in disparate sources and is dependent on advanced historical knowledge to fully analyze and interpret will not be as accessible to beginning students or students in a survey course.

Interweaving storytelling and document analysis is an engaging way of giving students the context they need to understand the sources and of providing them with motivation for analyzing documents. One of the challenges of teaching students the skills of doing history is that, outside of formal research projects, the motivation to analyze the sources is extrinsic—the instructor creates a graded analysis assignment and students perform the research in order to get a grade, not to answer an internally motivated research question. The intrinsic motivation—the desire to know—is one of the most thrilling parts of studying history, and it is difficult to replicate that thrill when the goal is to learn how to analyze historical sources, not necessarily to answer a research question.

Lessons should be crafted around pauses to examine the evidence. Instructors should capitalize on the opportunity to stop the story at a particularly interesting and dramatic moment and then allow the students to figure out what happened next by examining sources.

In telling the story of how colonists experienced the American Revolution, the instructor might tell the story of John and Abigail Adams. The instructor could narrate to students about the smallpox plague that spread through the colonies in the midst of increasing tension with Britain. While John Adams was in Philadelphia plotting independence, Abigail Adams was in Massachusetts trying to decide whether to inoculate their children against smallpox. The instructor could explain that catching the disease was a horrifying prospect, but inoculation was a relatively new and risky procedure.

Then, instead of simply telling the class what Abigail Adams decided to do, the instructor could pose some questions to the class: What should she do? How should she make a decision that will affect their whole family's future? How much input did John Adams have in the decision? Rather than answering the questions in a lecture, the instructor can then guide students through an examination of the Adamses' letters.

As the students dig through the letters, they can also evaluate what is possible to know or not know about Abigail Adams's thought process. They can consider what other sources would be valuable to help historians understand this moment. Had she lost relatives to smallpox? Based on the dates of the letters, did John Adams help his wife decide what to do? If it is possible to know, what were the rates of smallpox infection in the area at the time? What does this story tell us about women's lives during the revolutionary era?

In this approach, the compelling story—not the instructor's threat of low grades—provides the reason to carefully analyze the documents. The instructor has an opportunity to use the natural human curiosity to find out what happens next to provide students with a reason to analyze documents accurately. Choosing intriguing sources and crafting accurate narratives around those sources can pay off generously as students do history, not for a grade but in order to answer a research question (i.e., "How can we be sure of what happened next?").

Curating an opportunity for students to experience the thrill of answering a research question through interpreting sources brings students closer to the real work of historians. It uncovers the process of historical thinking, particularly how understanding and analyzing context, causality, and contingency helps historians tell this story more accurately and determine what questions remain.

Students can analyze documents for more than just the facts. As students become more adept in their skills, the instructor can introduce sources that provide ambiguous answers or can be interpreted in contradictory ways. For example, in telling stories from the early modern era, the instructor can introduce historical artifacts rather than written documents and challenge students to fill in the lives of members of early modern society based on items they made or valued. Students will likely come up with different interpretations, and that section of the story will remain ambiguous. The instructor should emphasize that ambiguity is part of the interpretation of the past.

As the instructor returns to the story itself, she should give students opportunities to ask questions and evaluate the facts. Either at the end of the story or at key moments throughout, the instructor should lead a discussion or offer a writing prompt to challenge students to think through the contingency and complexity evident in the story. Why did events happen the way they did? What contingencies shaped the narrative? What complexities influenced the main character's choices? How would the story change if the focus was on a different main character? Given our analyses of the historical record, how certain are the facts? What other sources are needed to complete the story?

Leaving time to contemplate these questions is critical to using stories effectively. Instructors might be tempted to get caught up in the fun of telling a good story and to be seen as an omniscient storyteller. This does a disservice to students, however, by making them think that the outcome of the story is inevitable, that the story is completely knowable, or that the story represents all people and events from that time. Breaking down the story shows the role of choice and contingency and the difficulties of interpreting the past through source analyses. The lesson is much richer if the story is not only told but interrogated.

Using two or more stories to compare and contrast is another way to hold interest and present multiple perspectives. The stories of two people living in the same place but leading very different lives, for example, can help students broaden their understanding of a particular society. The stories of two national leaders confronting the same crisis in different ways can help students compare and contrast political approaches. Even the stories of two generals facing the same battle can help students view events through multiple lenses. And, of course, in keeping with the approach, students can analyze documents representing the two stories and determine how the primary source information contributes to the story.

Biography as Story

The most straightforward source for stories comes from biographies.[16] Telling the story of a person's life and how they affected and were affected by key events can easily make the abstract personal and compelling. Instructors may easily adapt biographies for classroom use if the sources are plentiful and accessible. In addition, there may be an abundance of personal primary sources such as letters, diaries, personal writings, and photographs that allow students to explore the inner life of the subject. While complexities of interpretation still exist, a biography is often easily relatable since students are also navigating a life in society in the same way as the subject once did.

Biographies are also a useful lens for storytelling because they can illuminate a previously marginalized figure or add complexity to a well-known biography. For example, telling the story of a battle from the perspective of a woman working as a camp follower can "cover" the battle while also decentering the narrative. As students invest in the woman's story, they see the social effects of military action.

Similarly, telling the story of a tangentially famous person can provide a unique window onto the more well-known figure's experience. For instance, discussing Andrew Jackson's political career from the viewpoint of his wife, Rachel Donelson Robards Jackson, opens up the discussion of the public's perception of Jackson and the costs of his political ambition. Likewise, discussing the connection between women's rights and abolition through the perspective of Theodore Weld (the mentor and later spouse of Angelina Grimké) shows the complexity of the fight for equality. Using a famous-adjacent person can also cover more content as it illuminates not only the well-known person or event but also the social and cultural milieu in which they lived.

Stories can also make abstract concepts concrete. A bullet point lecture about nineteenth-century European Protestant religious belief is likely to be mind-numbingly dull, but the story of British Protestant missionary James Peggs's understanding of how his religious convictions should shape his actions is intriguing. Information about nineteenth-century European Protestant belief can be interwoven with the lived experience of the missionary. The content is not sacrificed in the interest of telling a story; rather, it is applied directly. Students, therefore, are constantly seeing how and why historical literacy (i.e., factual knowledge) is useful because it allows them to understand real-life experiences more deeply.

It is worth reiterating that using stories goes beyond plugging in real people or events as examples to illuminate general information. The point of using stories is to bring students closer to the real work of historians and to allow them to experience, in real time, how general information helps them interpret the historical record. In that sense, using stories allows students to constantly compare specific experiences with the broad metanarrative and think about how general facts are derived from historical sources. This provides students with a much richer version of history than a series of guided notes copied from a slide presentation.

A potential downside to using biographies as the focus of the lesson is that it brings up the question of whether it is useful, or even possible, to generalize from such a specific story. Considering the example of the Protestant missionary, James Peggs, the question arises: Did he actually practice orthodox Protestant belief or was his experience so anomalous as to hardly be categorized as Protestant? If the latter, the risk is that students will remember the particularities of James Peggs and forget that he was not representative of mainstream Protestant belief. This potential downside reinforces the need to (1) choose biographies wisely in order to align with the goals of the lesson, (2) use primary sources to provide necessary context, and (3) consider using more than one story to add complexity to each narrative.

Example by Comparison

Consider three ways of presenting a lesson on Westward Expansion in a U.S. History survey class. In the first approach, the instructor displays a slide presentation with the following information, which students copy word for word:

1. Westward Expansion (1807–1910)
    a. Homestead Act (1862)
    b. California Gold Rush (1848–1855)
    c. Oregon and California Trails
    d. Transcontinental Railroad
        i. Completed 1869
        ii. Promontory, Utah
    e. Battle of Little Bighorn (1876)
        i. Custer's Last Stand
    f. Dawes Act (1887)
        i. Federal government authorized to break up tribal lands
        ii. Assimilation

As students are copying the slides, the instructor reads each word on the slides and perhaps adds in a few more facts about each bullet point. The students mainly ignore the instructor as they copy the slides and then disengage. The instructor might then continue the lesson with slides about the development of the American West or perhaps play an instructional video that repeats many of the bullet points from the slides. Neither the instructor nor the students muster up much enthusiasm for this set of facts, but the instructor is relieved that she "covered" so much material in one lesson.

A second approach provides a comparison. The instructor begins by announcing, "Today I am going to tell you a story. As I do, think about this question: Why did Americans go west? Jot down some information that will help you answer this question, and we will try to answer it at the end. Our story starts with a man named Uriah Oblinger."[17] The instructor proceeds to tell the story of the Oblinger family, showing students letters written by Uriah Oblinger and his family members and maps and photographs to illustrate the Oblingers' journeys around the West as their family grows.

As she tells the story, the instructor weaves in all of the facts from the slide presentation above, but only as they naturally arise in the Oblingers' story. For example, when Uriah Oblinger, desperate to make money, takes a job working for the railroad, the instructor can discuss the importance of the transcontinental railroad to the development of the West. Students can compare maps showing the spread of railway lines over time. After this detour, the story resumes. The slide presentation shows pictures of the Oblingers but also could display many of the relevant facts and dates to help students develop their answer to the initial question.

The instructor pauses the story periodically to ask questions that check for understanding or to allow students to read and analyze relevant documents, particularly to bring in perspectives that are different from the main character's experience. For example, to supplement the Oblingers' story, students can analyze Chief Joseph's 1877 testimony to the U.S. government regarding broken treaties and white Americans' westward expansion or images of Chinese laborers in California.

At the end, the instructor leads students through a verbal or written exercise to respond to the question posed at the beginning of class. Then, for the rest of the course, the students and teacher can use their exploration of the Oblingers' story as shorthand for their collective memory about the development of the West. Not only is the story a more memorable way to learn, it also builds classroom community much more effectively than the one-way transfer of facts from slides to student.

Focusing on a biography is not the only way to do it, however. A third approach is evident in how historians have cast new light on well-known events by filtering them through commodity studies or examining the history of institutions and how they change over time.[18]

For instance, while the words "postal geography" do not necessarily seem like something that will grab students' attention, historian Cameron Blevins uses data visualization to show how the expansion of post offices across the American West opens a new way of understanding westward expansion. He is able to use data points to craft a story about the expansion of and resistance to state power in the West. His digital humanities work, coupled with the easily accessible ephemera available online through the National Postal Museum, provides a rich set of resources for instructors to craft a story about westward expansion and for students to interact with maps, graphs, and artifacts.[19]

Again, the story of the post office and westward expansion would still cover all of the bullet points from the original slide presentation, but they would be embedded into a story that both students and instructor are constructing and actively engaging with. The emphasis is on the practice of history rather than listing facts for later memorization.

When using stories, it can be tempting to make up a historically plausible story. Instead of digging into the story of the spread of post offices across the West, why not spin an action-packed yarn about a theoretical Pony Express rider, encountering adventure and danger on his route across the prairie? While the teacher might have students on the edge of their seats, the students will quickly disengage when the instructor tells them that the story is fictional, or, perhaps worse, they will remember the fiction as fact because it is more interesting than the dry lesson.

History does not need embellishment. Stories that are grounded in documentary evidence and historical context can be utterly fascinating and attention-sustaining. Instructors must resist the temptation to tell made-up or even composite stories because students are best served when instructors give them opportunities to build both historical literacy and historical thinking. That skill-building goal is why instructors must maintain strict historical accuracy, make note of where there are questions in the record, explain what is possible and not possible to know, and pause the story occasionally to have students analyze documents themselves.

Like the other approaches outlined in this book, this strategy can be duplicated over and over. While using stories in the same way for every lesson would get boring, having this approach as a template to be repeated throughout the course gives the instructor a starting point for crafting the lesson. In addition, repeating the stories approach throughout the course allows students to sharpen their skills through repetition. Finally, the stories can give the class a shared narrative that they can draw upon throughout the class.

CUSTOMIZE

While the approach outlined in this chapter focuses on strict historical accuracy in using stories, there are a number of ways to adapt the approach to keep its essential features while also making it one's own. One adjacent idea to the approach outlined here is to use historical fiction, meaning novels or short stories, as the attention-cultivating basis for the lesson.[20]

There are many benefits to using historical fiction as the foundational story upon which to build content knowledge. The right text can be immersive, engaging, and even teach historical content, if the author prioritized historical accuracy. Instructors can choose between texts written during the time period or modern texts that look back.

For example, Jules Verne's *Around the World in Eighty Days* was published in 1873, near the height of European imperialism. In addition to being an engaging and fun adventure story, the novel is a product of its time and therefore illuminates the worldview and values of European imperialists. In that way, instructors can use the book as a primary source as well as a way to immerse students in the historical time period.

A classic example of a more modern work of fiction that looks back at a historical time period is Art Spiegelman's *Maus I: A Survivor's Tale: My Father Bleeds History* (1986). The book is a graphic novelization of the author's interviews with his father, a Holocaust survivor. The book opens discussions about oral history and the creation of narratives as well as the interplay of art and stories. It provides a powerful window into a topic that can be difficult to grasp due to the sheer scope of the horror.

From using written fiction, it can be a short step to using other forms of mass media, especially movies and television shows. A movie can be a relatively fast way to tell a powerful story and to help students visualize a time period. The difficulty can be that the return to history-as-text can feel like a loss in momentum and interest. Movies and television shows are also not inherently interactive. Students do not have to use their imaginations to picture the story and instead passively absorb it. Even a postmovie discussion can feel like an afterthought. On the other hand, a film can be a way to give the class a common story to use as a touchpoint for deeper historical research.

There are many other ways that instructors can adapt stories or story sources. There are many robust online repositories of oral histories.[21] While the stories may not be concise, comparing several—or even many—oral histories can allow the class to construct a narrative of an event based on diverse points of view. In some ways, building a story out of diverse sources is the opposite of using a single story as the foundation for content knowledge, but the approach would allow students to put previously acquired content knowledge to work in weeding through and making sense of the oral histories. The approach is limited, of course, to the fairly recent past when oral histories began to be collected.

Another angle on using stories is to use local history or ancestry history as the source for stories. This is a way of incorporating physical archives that are nearby, either through a field trip or by inviting an archivist or preservationist into the classroom. The stories might be more object- or location-based, such as telling the story of a farm through several generations. Many historic sites already present local history as the stories of individuals, and tapping into those stories can give students an opportunity to do historical work differently from relying on digitized sources. Of course, the instructor must work to make connections between local stories and the broad metanarrative, perhaps through comparing several stories or assigning additional context readings.

The onus for finding stories does not need to be all on the instructor. Students can find stories as part of a research project and present their stories to the class. The easiest way of doing this is through biography and having students present biographical reports on historical figures. Allowing students to choose from a list gives them some agency while also ensuring coverage. Including a requirement that students find and analyze one or more relevant primary sources also reinforces the connection between the documentary record and the construction of stories.

Rather than having all students present on their biography subjects at once, the reports can be spread out throughout the course to provide an anchor or touchstone story for that week's lessons. Instructors can actively refer to the students' presentations to demonstrate that the class is working together to construct an understanding of the history. The instructor can also point out how the students' choices about presenting the narrative influence the class's understanding of the time period.

CONCLUSION

This chapter outlined an approach to telling stories that builds on recent pedagogical and historical scholarship that explores the benefits of using stories to maintain students' attention and as an entry point into dense historical content. The chapter discussed how to put the approach into practice by finding useable stories, telling the stories in an engaging way, and interweaving primary sources and content knowledge into the stories.

With this approach, students construct and deconstruct stories, learning and experiencing the limits of the documentary record and of narrative as a form of history. As with the other approaches outlined so far, the goal is for students and instructor to join together in a project of building communal understanding of history. While valuing the application of content knowledge to understanding and interpreting stories, the approach eschews bullet-point slide presentations in favor of engaging and enriching stories and story-based analysis activities. Students, therefore, do history even as they learn and interact with a memorable narrative.

SAMPLE STORY-BASED LESSON OUTLINE

I. Introduce topic and story
    a. Explain guiding question
    b. Explain student responsibilities and goals
II. Tell story
    a. Narrative

  b. Pause for questions and discussions related to complexity and contingency
  c. Narrative
  d. Pause for document analysis and discussion of causality
  e. Narrative
III. Conclusion
  a. Discussion of how historical thinking aids in understanding the story more deeply
  b. Discussion of guiding question
  c. Discussion of remaining questions and ideas on how to find answers

NOTES

1. It is hardly new to decry the boring lecture, which some might contend is simply a straw man argument. See Doug Lemov, "A Vast Army of Terracotta Warriors: Just How Do We Teach History?" *Teach Like a Champion* (blog), January 16, 2014, https://teachlikeachampion.org/blog/vast-army-terracotta-warriors-just-teach-history/. Yet for underprepared or overworked teachers, the coverage model is particularly alluring and persistent. See Dave Eaton, "Taking Cover: Explaining the Persistence of the Coverage Model in World History Surveys," *World History Connected*, February 2016, accessed March 21, 2023, https://worldhistoryconnected.press.uillinois.edu/13.1/eaton.html.

2. Debra Hamel, *Trying Neaira: The True Story of a Courtesan's Scandalous Life in Ancient Greece* (New Haven, CT: Yale University Press, 2003).

3. Lendol Calder, "The Stories We Tell," *OAH Magazine of History* 27, no. 3 (2013): 5–8.

4. Steven R. Corman, "The Difference between Story and Narrative," Center for Strategic Communication, Arizona State University, March 21, 2013, https://csc.asu.edu/2013/03/21/the-difference-between-story-and-narrative/.

5. Jennifer Frost, "Using 'Master Narratives' to Teach History: The Case of the Civil Rights Movement," *The History Teacher* 45, no. 3 (2012): 437–46.

6. Clare Hake and Terry Haydn, "Stories or Sources?" *Teaching History*, no. 78 (1995): 20.

7. Diane Ketelle, "Introduction to the Special Issue: What Is Storytelling in the Higher Education Classroom?" *Storytelling, Self, Society* 13, no. 2 (2017): 144–45.

8. James Lang, *Distracted: Why Students Can't Focus and What You Can Do about It* (New York: Basic Books, 2020), 149, 153.

9. Gabriel McNett, "Using Stories to Facilitate Learning," *College Teaching* 64, no. 4 (2016): 185, https://doi.org/10.1080/87567555.2016.1189389. See also Grant Bage, *Narrative Matters: Teaching History through Story* (London: Routledge, 1999); and John E. Wills, Jr., "Lives and Other Stories: Neglected Aspects of the Teacher's Art," *The History Teacher* 26, no. 1 (1992): 33–49, https://doi.org/10.2307/494084.

10. McNett, "Using Stories," 190.

11. Fred Anderson and Andrew Cayton, "The Problem of Authority in the Writing of Early American History," *The William and Mary Quarterly* 66, no. 3 (2009): 471.

12. David Gerwin and Jack Zevin. *Teaching U. S. History as Mystery*, 2nd ed. (New York: Routledge, 2011); Jack Zevin and David Gerwin, *Teaching World History as Mystery* (New York: Routledge, 2010).

13. For some discussion of this complex topic, see David Carr, *Time, Narrative, and History* (Bloomington: Indiana University Press, 1986); Mark Freeman, "Narrative as a Mode of Understanding: Method, Theory, Praxis," in *The Handbook of Narrative Analysis*, ed. Anna De Fina and Alexandra Georgakopoulou (West Sussex, UK: John Wiley & Sons, 2015), 21–38; Crispin Sartwell, *End of Story: Toward an Annihilation of Language and History* (Albany: State University of New York Press, 2000).

14. Bruce Robbins, "Commodity Histories," *PMLA* 120, no. 2 (2005): 454–63; see the Animal Series available from Reaktion Books at https://reaktionbooks.co.uk/series/animal (accessed July 4, 2023).

15. More on Aiko Herzig-Yoshinaga's story can be found at Jennifer Hill, "Inventory of Aiko Herzig Yoshinaga Papers," Online Archive of California, October 31, 2019, https://oac.cdlib.org/findaid/ark:/13030/c8kp888m/entire_text/.

16. Biography as a starting point for history has elicited a rich discussion in the historiography. See Lois W. Banner, "Biography as History," *The American Historical Review* 114, no. 3 (2009): 579–86; Robert I. Rotberg, "Biography and Historiography: Mutual Evidentiary and Interdisciplinary Considerations," *The Journal of Interdisciplinary History* 40, no. 3 (2010): 305–24; Susan Ware, "Writing Women's Lives: One Historian's Perspective," *The Journal of Interdisciplinary History* 40, no. 3 (2010): 413–35.

17. Library of Congress and Nebraska State Historical Society, "About the Letters from the Uriah W. Oblinger Collection," Prairie Settlement: Nebraska Photographs and Family Letters, accessed May 17, 2023, https://memory.loc.gov/ammem/award98/nbhihtml/aboutoblinger.html.

18. See for example Mark Kurlansky, *Salt: A World History* (New York: Penguin Books, 2003).

19. Cameron Blevins, *Paper Trails: The US Post and the Making of the American West* (New York: Oxford University Press, 2021). See also Cameron Blevins, "Postal Geography and the Golden West" (blog post), October 30, 2014, https://www.cameronblevins.org/posts/postal-geography-and-the-golden-west/; Smithsonian Institution, National Postal Museum, accessed July 3, 2023, https://postalmuseum.si.edu/.

20. See the discussions in Katherine Aiken, "Superhero History: Using Comic Books to Teach U.S. History," *OAH Magazine of History* 24, no. 2 (2010): 41–47; Benjamin J. J. Leff, "Popular Culture as Historical Text: Using Mass Media to Teach American History," *The History Teacher* 50, no. 2 (2017): 227–54; Grant Rodwell, *Whose History? Engaging History Students through Historical Fiction* (Adelaide: University of Adelaide Press, 2013); Kevin Vanzant, "Problems with

Narrative in the U.S. Survey and How Fiction Can Help," *The History Teacher* 52, no. 4 (2019): 677–96.

21. A good place to start is the Oral History Association, https://oralhistory.org/, which keeps a list of oral history centers and collections (accessed July 3, 2023).

Chapter 5

Visual Literacies

Students huddle around maps of the world created in the 1500s. The conversation pings with questions and comments. "What's that huge island in the Pacific?" "What's that extra part west of California?" "Everything is so far north!" "Can you read that description? What language is it?" "Antarctica is gigantic!" As they explore and compare the maps, the students start to recognize that even an image as seemingly authoritative as a map is a representation of a perspective that includes layers of meaning and interpretation.

The students in the example were fumbling toward understanding the complexities of interpreting images, or "visual literacy." Rather than leaving students to muddle through, instructors can capitalize on the accessibility of images to help students analyze, question, and deconstruct visual representations of past events, ideas, people, and eras—in short, to develop visual literacy.

Despite the importance of visual literacy, many instructors without an advanced art degree may feel ill-equipped to incorporate images in history instruction beyond their use as illustration. Because of these limitations, instructors might underutilize images, particularly when it comes to challenging students to practice historical analysis skills and develop historical thinking. Nevertheless, by accessing a variety of strategies to use and analyze images, instructors can teach visual literacy, even without being an expert in images.

Photographs may be the most accessible images for classroom use, and many pedagogical scholars have examined and initiated projects to utilize photograph analysis in class. The scholarly conversation surrounding photographs and historical thinking and skills is particularly vibrant. This chapter builds on that discussion by applying many of those principles not only to photographs but also to any source that helps students develop visual literacy.[1]

This chapter focuses on photographs, artwork (including paintings, prints, drawings, etchings, and sculptures), cartoons, advertisements, posters, maps, and images of historical objects. Even so, the same principles apply, perhaps with some adaptation, to interpreting and understanding a wide range of visuals including tables, graphs, charts, infographics, plans and blueprints, the built environment, video games, clothing, and more.

IN THEORY

The theoretical underpinning of this approach is a recognition of the importance of visual literacy as both a twenty-first-century skill and a foundational skill for historians. The Association of College & Research Libraries defines visual literacy as "a set of abilities that enables an individual to effectively find, interpret, evaluate, use, and create images and visual media. Visual literacy skills equip a learner to understand and analyze the contextual, cultural, ethical, aesthetic, intellectual, and technical components involved in the production and use of visual materials."[2] The aspects of visual literacy that are particularly relevant to developing historical thinking include the ability to "interpret, evaluate, [and] use" images.

A more recent development within scholarship on visual literacy is the relevance—especially for history instruction—of "critical visual literacy." This approach challenges the reader to search for "hidden messages, ideologies, and power interests behind the information conveyed as part of larger social, historical, and political contexts."[3] The goal of critical visual literacy is not simply to interpret an image within its historical context but rather to take the analysis a step further and "illuminate the power relationships in society" with the goal of guiding students to use their "creative voices to promote an equal, democratic society."[4] The basic components of visual literacy therefore provide a foundation for more critical analysis of the power dynamics included in the production, distribution, and reception of images. As students become more skilled in multiple visual literacies, they can consider how images add complexity to their own research and reckoning with the past.[5]

Unpacking these ideas and applying them to the classroom necessitates evaluating how historical thinking and skills blend with the standards for visual literacy. Instructors can use familiar skills such as discerning authorship, context, and interconnections; utilizing close reading; and researching multiple perspectives as the starting point for developing visual literacy. Then, teachers can build on these strategies to account for the ways that visuals differ from texts.[6]

Because images are accessible, especially at first glance, students are often more comfortable offering their own interpretations than they are when faced with text. Nevertheless, students need guidance to make connections between the historical context and content that they know and are learning in class with their interpretation of images. The danger comes from the temptation to offer "relatively simplistic emotional interpretations" of images, particularly when they are disconnected from other images, documents, or context.[7] Instructors must train students to place images in context and to put the images in conversation with other historical and scholarly sources.

Once students are equipped to understand images, the next step is to use images effectively to answer historical questions and support arguments. The basic approach to utilizing images is the same for using documents. That method includes recognizing that, like texts, "pictures are frequently not attempts at realistic representation, but rather are carefully constructed spaces, using symbols and allusions to convey complex messages."[8] Although the questions might differ from those used for text, the goal of understanding and interrogating a time, place, group, or idea is the same as for other types of sources.[9]

On the other hand, images are different from textual documents, and they can and should be used differently. For one, photographs can grab attention and quickly engage students. Photographs also "trigger emotional responses" that might not occur from reading a description of the pictured event.[10] Finally, images can represent and offer multiple perspectives, particularly perspectives that might not be available via text. As students deconstruct the exercise of power inherent in a created image, they can work toward more nuanced arguments that make use of multiple readings of images.

Many instructors might be comfortable with using the principles of visual literacy with photographs, paintings, and other works of art; however, maps and images of artifacts present additional challenges and opportunities.[11] Many instructors are familiar with using maps as illustrations but might overlook the possibilities for deeper analysis. Scholars note that, like photographs, maps provide information in an accessible form, particularly if instructors equip students with some basic map-reading skills. Because maps "encapsulate not only geographic knowledge but also the scientific, technological, and intellectual knowledge of an era" historical maps in particular can provide a valuable window into a time, place, and worldview.[12]

Maps, like other images, can give students opportunities to learn "how to evaluate evidence, how to look closely, how to weigh differing interpretations, and how to see change over time."[13] Nevertheless, many students see maps the same way they see text in a textbook—as authoritative and uncontested. Teaching students that all maps make arguments, leave out information, and reflect biases helps students see maps as akin to other historical images and texts. Students can also start to see all images as created and reflective of a particular time period and viewpoint.[14]

Images are useful because they represent a version of reality that students can explore more deeply through examination and historical questioning. In the same way, historical objects and artifacts have the power to reanimate the past.[15] Most teachers, however, have limited access to physical objects. While even that limited access should not be discounted, the widespread availability of high-resolution digital photographs of historical artifacts presents an intriguing compromise. Although a photograph of a historical artifact is different from other types of historical photographs, many of the close-reading questions necessary to understand and use images can be applied to object pictures, with some adjustment.

Scholars have developed creative and useful ways of bringing images into the classroom.[16] Even so, teachers should prioritize advancing students' historical thinking skills in any image-based activity. Because photographs, maps, and artwork grab attention and are open to interpretation, instructors might feel that their students have learned well from any analysis of images. Nevertheless, instructors should not abandon the careful planning and scaffolding necessary to the development of historical thinking and critical evaluation, no matter the medium.

IN PRACTICE

Instructors trained in text-based historical analysis may feel intimidated by the prospect of teaching visual literacy, if only for the sheer number of visual types available to historians, particularly in the digital age. Keeping in mind the goals of teaching students to (1) understand images, both literally and critically, and (2) use images effectively to make arguments and answer research questions helps to guide the practical steps teachers can take to incorporate images into history instruction, even if they need to occasionally act as co-learners with students. This section explores that role for teachers as well as teaching strategies related to both understanding and using images.

Instructor as Co-Learner

While using available resources to develop skills can help a novice instructor feel confident, there are also benefits to acting as co-learners with students. Inviting students to join the teacher in stumbling through an interpretation and then doing research to answer remaining questions helps students see the process of historical interpretation in action and how intriguing it is. It may be necessary for the teacher to inform students that she is taking on the role of co-learner for the purpose of joint discovery. Students may need guidance in seeing the instructor in this different role.

Visuals present this opportunity in a unique way because issues of interpretation are not tied to vocabulary or reading skills as is the case when interpreting documents. It is harder for instructors to demonstrate "stumbling through" an interpretation of a document that is also accessible to students; through repeated exposure, trained historians expect that words will have multiple meanings and uses and that the writing skills of the author can clarify and/or obscure the text's meaning.

When faced with an image, however, instructors might instinctively know that there is more than meets the eye, but they might not know exactly what it is. Joining students as co-learners in visual literacy and critical evaluation helps students see that they can develop skills through practice. Even if teachers do not feel confident in fully interpreting any image, they can still put structures in place to help the classroom community develop the necessary skills.

The teacher's mindset is the first structure that must be in place. Although the instructor may not feel fully visually literate, he can still be the expert in the room on historical context and make that role clear to students. Grounding images in historical context changes image examination from appreciation to analysis. The teacher must continually lead students to consider the context and use the visual clues to establish the historical reality.

While the instructor should be the expert on historical context, he should also recognize the opportunity to bring in experts who are more visually literate. A curator or archivist from a local historic site can visit the class and provide a lesson on visual literacy. Or the class can work through video and website resources that teach visual literacy. The point is for the instructor to position herself as a co-learner and show students how to gain necessary skills. Even with additional training, instructors need to demonstrate to students that visual literacy involves ambiguity, multiple interpretations, and lingering questions.

Understanding Images

While there are many facets to visual literacy, in the context of history and social studies there are several elements that instructors must prioritize to equip students to both understand and use images. To start, the three main facets of understanding images include (1) deciphering the components, (2) evaluating the implications of context and sourcing, and (3) analyzing argument or perspective. Practicing these skills of understanding will equip students to then be able to use visuals effectively to make arguments and answer research questions.

Deciphering Components

Students can practice the foundational skill of understanding the components of an image in several ways. Scholars have developed questions and activities to help students understand the components of images; many of the questions revolve around encouraging students to slow down and look more closely.[17] Questions to help students decipher the individual parts of an image might include the following:

1. What do you see at first glance?
2. Look closer. What elements do you notice that you missed at first? What is in the background and foreground? What elements are easy or difficult to decipher?
3. What is the focus of the image? What did the creator want you to see?
4. What is left out of this image?
5. What questions do you have about the image? How might you answer them?

There are many more questions that could be considered along these same lines, particularly depending on the students' skill levels. Teachers can apply these questions and others like them to photographs, artwork, and historical maps, perhaps with some adjustment. There are benefits to using the same or similar questions each time the class analyzes an image. Students begin to recognize that all historical images are created and represent a particular point of view or message from the creator. Once students understand what is included in an image, they can start to think about why the creator made it.

Photographs of historical objects are a somewhat special class of visual sources; nevertheless, they warrant the same close examination that other images require. Similar to other images, at first glance a photo of an object may seem fairly straightforward, but taking time for close examination and generating questions will allow the viewer to gain more information from the object. In addition, many museum and historic site websites that present images of the objects in their collection also provide information about the objects. Sometimes the information only includes the date, creator, and materials, but other times the provided historical context can be extensive.[18]

Evaluating Context and Sourcing

Interpreting images in context is key to building understanding of an image. There are three types of contexts to draw students' attention to: historical, source, and historiographical. Some context questions might include the following:

1. When was this image created?
2. Think about the general topic of the image. What relevant events occurred before and after this image?
3. How would people at the time the image was created perceive or think about this image? Why?
4. Who created this image? What do we know about their worldview and work?
5. Why did they create it? How do we know?

One way instructors can help students practice this skill of grounding images in historical context is to give them an image without a date and simply ask them to guess the year in which it was created. Depending on the image, students may be able to get to the exact date, or they might be decades off. The instructor can then walk the students through the visual clues that are present (clothing styles, technology, physical setting, photograph technology, etc.) and how they connect to historical events and time periods. Instructors can also challenge students to find other images that the instructor and students can attempt to date together.

It is also important for students to think about the source context of an image, whether by examining images by the same creator or from the same historical moment. In the same way that understanding one document is greatly enhanced if put in conversation with other documents, understanding images increases if they are analyzed in the context of other images. A famous example is Dorothea Lange's *Migrant Mother* (1936), which is one of several exposures Lange took of the same subject.[19] For historical maps, examining several maps created around the same time helps to contextualize the source of the map students are working to interpret.

The process of understanding source context is a useful opportunity for students to find related images themselves. The instructor can either provide several websites with relevant image collections or help students think through relevant search terms. To widen the source set, the instructor might require that each student or group finds a different image. This contextualization work will likely help to answer other understanding questions or could generate even more questions.

As students think through source context, the instructor can challenge them to evaluate power dynamics inherent in the image and its creation. Asking questions such as "Did the subjects consent to or participate in the creation of this image?" or "What factors motivated the creator to make this image?" can guide students to use multiple visual literacies to view and understand the image. Although these questions can still apply if the author of the image is unknown, the instructor should emphasize that answers will be speculative.

A third area of context involves examining the relevant historiography. While it is an excellent learning experience for students to progress through asking and answering questions about images, the instructor should also guide students through the conversation historians are having about either the image, the topic, or both. Even though not every photograph, painting, and historical map has a robust scholarly discussion surrounding it, many do, and even more so, the specific topic of the image is likely of interest to historians.

For example, the photo in figure 5.1, titled *Junior Normal Class of Fisk University, Nashville, Tennessee, Seated on Steps Outside of Building*, dated between 1890 and 1906, might not have generated the full scholarly conversation that surrounds a Pulitzer prize–winning photograph.[20] However, both Fisk University and Black women's education between 1890 and 1906 are the subject of much historiographical discussion.

While the instructor will likely want students to generate their own conversation in the exploration phase, giving them relevant excerpts from scholarly sources, showing a video interview with a historian or exploring a website created by historians can help instructors show students how images fit into historiographical discussions. Pointing students to the scholarly debate is more useful for the development of historical skills than the instructor providing a consensus of the discussion without attributing historians. Students see

Figure 5.1. Junior Normal Class of Fisk University, Nashville, Tennessee, Seated on Steps Outside of Building.
Library of Congress Prints and Photographs Division, https://www.loc.gov/item/94513859/.

that they are entering a conversation, rather than simply viewing illustrations of an established narrative.

Recognizing and Interrogating Argument

Teaching students to understand the perspective and purpose of an image's creator is another key skill in understanding images and a vital step toward exercising critical visual literacy. Nevertheless, unless the creator included a written description of their goals and ideas, it can be difficult to answer all questions related to the author's argument or purpose in creating the image. Joining together as a class to tease out the ideas behind the image helps to develop important historical thinking skills and leads to deeper analyses of purpose and power.

Some foundational questions include the following:

1. How did the author create the image? If people are included, is it posed or candid? How can you tell?
2. (For photographs and artwork of people in particular) how would the subject of the image perceive the image if they saw it?
3. How did the creator want this image to be used? How do you know?
4. Who was the intended audience and how might they have received it? How might an unintended audience perceive it?
5. (For photographs and maps in particular) what is left out? What is left in? Why?

The questions should generate discussion, even if firm answers may be difficult to come by. The instructor should be clear that answers to the questions may exist with further research. In some instances, the instructor may wish to become an expert on an image and then explain the research process to students. However, if the instructor has all the answers for every image examined in class, students might be more reluctant to offer their own ideas and interpretations. As noted earlier, there is some benefit to the teacher taking on the role of question-generator rather than image expert.

The goal is for students to recognize that photographs, maps, and artwork are all making some sort of argument or statement, and that they are providing one perspective on the world and excluding others.[21] Students can then move from identifying the argument to interrogating its function and authority. For example, the photo in figure 5.2 titled *Civil Rights March on Washington, D.C.*, dated August 28, 1963, has an argument or perspective that is fairly straightforward.[22]

That is, the people pictured were participating in a march for equal rights as Americans. Their signs list a number of civil rights that were contentious

Figure 5.2.   Civil Rights March on Washington, D.C. Warren K. Leffler, photographer.
Library of Congress Prints and Photographs Division, Washington, DC, https://lccn.loc.gov/2003654393.

issues in the 1960s. Most of the people in the photograph appear to be African Americans.

Students might observe that the photographer seemingly did not intend to depict the marchers in either a highly flattering or unflattering light. Still, the photographer did intentionally include the text of the signs, and most of the people in the foreground appear to be women. Students would likely reach a point in their questioning where identifying the marchers and/or the photographer would be the key to a nuanced interpretation. Teachers can reinforce the importance of unanswered questions and paths for additional research.

Just as photographers make many choices in what to display and how to display it, cartographers also include a selection of information, to the exclusion of other information. This principle is amplified when looking at historical maps. For example, the map from around 1760 in figure 5.3 titled *A Correct Map of the World Drawn from the Best Discoveries*[23] has an argument that most students would be able to grasp fairly quickly, even just from the title.

Students would likely notice quite easily that, although the cartographer asserts that the map is "correct," the map reflects the questions that still remained about the globe in 1760 more than it reflects accurate knowledge of the globe as we understand it today.

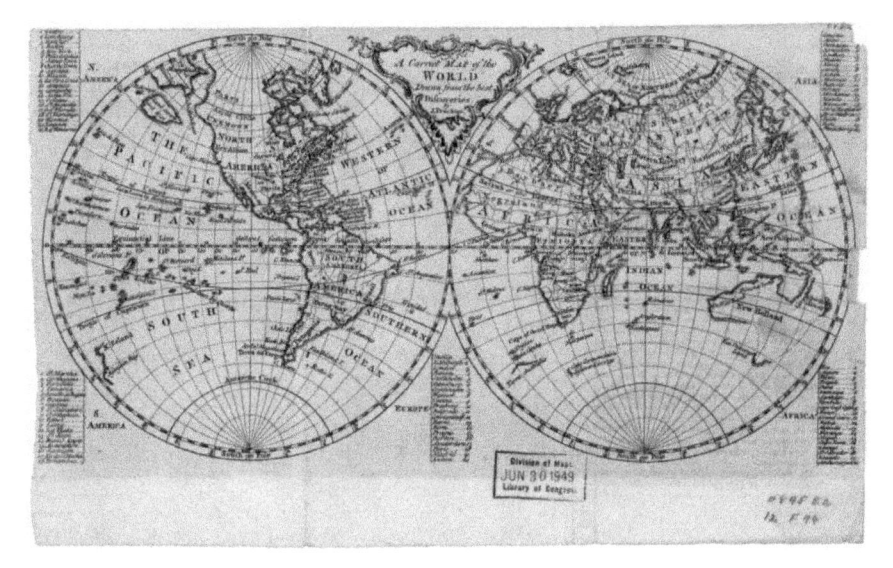

Figure 5.3. *A Correct Map of the World Drawn from the Best Discoveries*. J. Prockter, cartographer.
Library of Congress Geography and Map Division, Washington, DC, https://lccn.loc.gov/2003654393.

By contrast, students would need more time and context to decipher the map in figure 5.4, titled *Missionary Map of the World Showing Prevailing Religions of Its Various Nations and the Central Stations of All Protestant Missionary Societies*, dated from around 1902.[24]

While students might be able to quickly infer that the map represents a Protestant view of a world dominated by European imperialism, they will likely need additional prompting to examine the map beyond the information highlighted in the map key in order to notice the projection, the titles, and the areas of emphasis. While the map does provide information about Protestant missionaries' views of world religions, it also uses a map projection that makes the "Heathen" sections of the world most prominent, adding urgency to the missionaries' cause. Students must learn that, even beyond the text and the map key, the cartographer and the map are not objective.

Recognizing and dissecting the arguments that images make trains students to read images as historical sources that they can use to answer historical questions, not simply to provide information or illustration. Digging deeper by analyzing the creator's authoritative stance toward the subject gives students the tools to add nuance and perspective to their own use of images as they develop and support answers to historical questions.

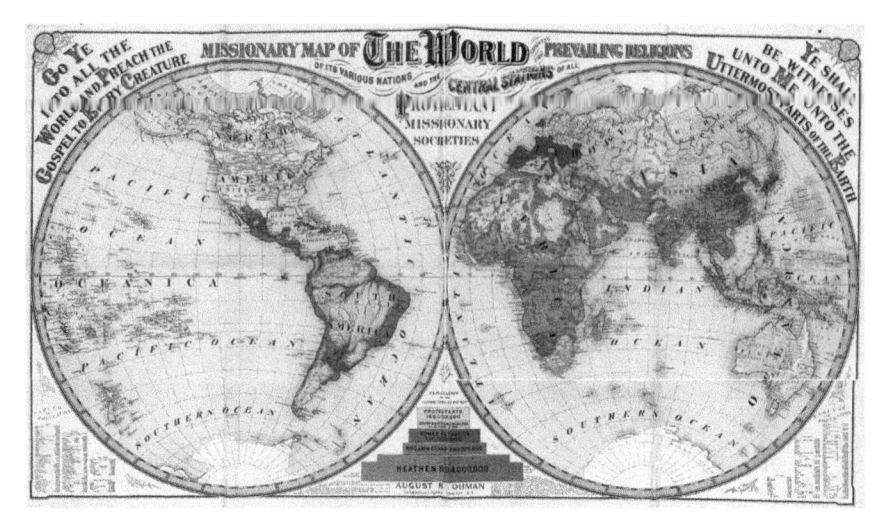

Figure 5.4. *Missionary Map of the World Showing Prevailing Religions of Its Various Nations and the Central Stations of All Protestant Missionary Societies.* August R. Ohman, cartographer.
Library of Congress Geography and Map Division, Washington, DC, https://www.loc.gov/item/2017586281/.

Using Images

After working through understanding images in various ways, students are ready to use visual sources to generate and answer research questions. One goal of visual literacy is the ability to use images accurately, which fits in well with the historical thinking skills of interpreting sources and making arguments about their significance.

There are several ways to teach students how to move past understanding a visual source and begin to use it for research purposes. One transition step in this process is to help students ask and answer questions based on more than one source. A jigsaw discussion can help students see the complexity that develops when several sources are analyzed together. Jigsaw discussions also help students write better research papers because they see the strength of an argument based on interpreting a set or related group of sources, rather than just one source.

The jigsaw discussion is a well-established strategy.[25] Briefly, it involves dividing students into groups and assigning each group a topic or source to investigate and become "experts" on. Each group then scatters to new groups made up of an expert from each topic. The students educate each other and create a group product that represents their learning. Endlessly adaptable, the jigsaw works very well for visual sources because groups can work together to understand images without periods of waiting silently as group members finish reading.

For example, for a jigsaw discussion about the development of women's participation in sports from 1900 to 1940, the instructor can give each group a different image, perhaps from different decades or perhaps all from the same year or any other variation. The students can work through image understanding prompts that encourage them to look closely at the image and think about its purpose. Then, students can scatter to their new groups, educate each other about their images, and respond to prompts that require them to use the images to answer historical evaluation and analysis questions and generate questions for further research. The goal of this activity is to push students to deeper levels of analysis even as they gain more content knowledge.

Another way to help students practice using images is to create a mystery for them to solve.[26] The activity works particularly well with images of objects, but photographs, artwork, and maps can also work. Document excerpts can also be included to give some context. The basic format is to give students a selection of sources with most or all of the identifying details (dates, locations, events, names) removed. The instructor can tell students that the sources connect to relay information about an event. Students will attempt to relate the objects to each other and form a hypothesis about the event. Then the instructor can progressively reveal more information and ask students to adjust their hypotheses. In the end, the teacher can challenge students to explain what questions are able to be answered about the event and what questions remain.

For instance, in an activity about the 1609–1610 "starving time" at Jamestown, the teacher would hand out images of artifacts that archaeologists have discovered at the Jamestown site as well as short excerpts from primary sources or historical maps of the colony without dates or location names. The teacher might give groups different sets of sources so that their theories differ and then challenge students to figure out what the crisis was and share their ideas. Then, the instructor reveals the dates and authors of the sources and prompts students to group the sources accordingly and revise their ideas. As the discussion develops and the instructor reveals more information, students revise their use of the images and recognize that some questions are unanswerable.

The purpose of reading images repeatedly through different lenses and perspectives is for even novice historians to engage deeply with the sources and have the skills to use images to answer research questions. Requiring students to demonstrate multiple visual literacies as they incorporate image analysis into their research projects or public history displays shows students why visual literacy is a potent tool in analyzing the past. Having a summative assessment that requires visual literacy in conjunction with historical thinking will reinforce for students that these skills are part of the necessary training for historians.

CUSTOMIZE

There are many ways to customize instruction in visual literacy to fit the content and students. It is important to consider whether students will best engage through verbal discussion or writing. Depending on the class size and maturity level, some classes will respond well to an open-ended discussion, with the instructor guiding students to visual literacy through questioning. Other classes will need the structure of written prompts or perhaps a more formal discussion that requires all students or groups to participate. Small group discussion, analysis, and written responses might be the best solution for very large classes, perhaps with the instructor offering periodic guidance or going over the answers at the end of the session.

Students can put their visual literacy and historical thinking skills to work in a variety of image-based summative assessments. There are many online tools that allow students to create curated displays of images and publish them online.[27] Projects that incorporate these resources give students the benefit of demonstrating visual literacy as well as teaching an audience how to understand and use images in the pursuit of historical knowledge.

Resources are also available to allow students to create their own maps based on historical content. These tools allow students to integrate historical sources, events, people, and ideas with locations, giving them a hands-on experience of mapping history and the opportunity to analyze how location affected historical events.[28] As students create their own maps, they can evaluate the choices they make as cartographers and explain how those decisions correspond to their argument about the content.

While there are some classes where practicing visual literacy is a secondary concern to other course goals, if reading images accurately is a focus of the course, then it should be included as a course objective or learning outcome. This helps both the student and the instructor work methodically toward achieving visual literacy through course activities and assessments. Spending time teaching students visual literacy is a worthwhile teaching strategy because the skills can be used again and again in class with many types of images—maps, objects, photographs, and artwork.

CONCLUSION

Visual literacy is an important element of historical thinking. Scholars recognize the power of art and photographs in grabbing students' attention and generating open-ended discussion. Keeping the main elements of visual literacy in mind should guide the teacher in the creation of image analysis exercises. The core components include teaching students to interpret, evaluate, and use images, while recognizing the importance of reading images through multiple lenses.

Understanding images includes deciphering the components, putting the images in historical, source, and historiographical context, and evaluating authorship and argument. As instructors join students as co-learners, they can demonstrate how visual literacy is developed and connects to historical thinking. Once students understand how to read and analyze images, they can use those skills to interpret sets of visual sources and answer research questions. Instructors can use many available digital tools to find images and allow students to research additional images. As teachers guide students to develop visual literacy, students can create projects that incorporate both visual literacy and historical thinking skills.

NOTES

1. A note on terminology: while photographs are generally considered works of art, for the purposes of this discussion, in this chapter photographs are distinguished from other works of "fine art." The term *artwork* will be used to refer especially to paintings and drawings, but other types of artwork (etchings, prints, collages, sculptures, etc.) would also be included.

2. American Library Association, "ACRL Visual Literacy Competency Standards for Higher Education," October 27, 2011, https://www.ala.org/acrl/standards/visualliteracy. See also Peter Felten, "Visual Literacy," *Change: The Magazine of Higher Learning* 40, no. 6 (2008): 60.

3. Melissa Schieble, "Reading Images in 'American Born Chinese' through Critical Visual Literacy," *The English Journal* 103, no. 5 (2014): 49.

4. Sheng Kuan Chung, "Critical Visual Literacy," *The International Journal of Arts Education* 11, no. 2 (2013): 6. See also Denise Newfield, "From Visual Literacy to Critical Visual Literacy: An Analysis of Educational Materials," *English Teaching: Practice and Critique* 10, no. 1 (2011): 81–94; Margaret Robbins, "Female Representation in Comics and Graphic Novels: Exploring Classroom Study with Critical Visual Literacy," *SIGNAL Journal* 38, no. 1 (2014): 11–15. The Association of College & Research Librarians incorporated many aspects of critical visual literacy into the "Companion Document to the ACRL Framework for Information Literacy for Higher Education," April 6, 2022, https://www.ala.org/acrl/sites/ala.org.acrl/files/content/standards/Framework_Companion_Visual_Literacy.pdf.

5. Dipti Desai, Jessica Hamlin, and Rachel Mattson, *History as Art, Art as History: Contemporary Art and Social Studies Education* (New York: Routledge, 2009), 6; Jessica B. Schocker, "A Case for Using Images to Teach Women's History," *The History Teacher* 47, no. 3 (2014): 421, 426.

6. Sam Wineburg, "Thinking Like a Historian," *Teaching with Primary Sources Quarterly* 3, no. 1 (Winter 2010): 3. Wineburg's key components for interpreting

historical sources include "sourcing, contextualizing, close reading, using background knowledge, reading the silences, and corroborating."

7. David Jaffee, "Thinking Visually as Historians: Incorporating Visual Methods," in Michael Coventry et al., "Ways of Seeing: Evidence and Learning in the History Classroom," *Journal of American History* 92, no. 4 (2006): 1378.

8. Jane Card, "Picturing Place: What You Get May Be More Than What You See," *Teaching History* 116 (2004): 16. See also Anna Pegler-Gordon, "Seeing Images in History," *Perspectives on History: The Newsmagazine of the American Historical Association*, February 1, 2006, https://www.historians.org/research-and-publications/perspectives-on-history/february-2006/seeing-images-in-history; Bill Tally and Lauren B. Goldenberg, "Fostering Historical Thinking with Digitized Primary Sources," *Journal of Research on Technology in Education* 38, no. 1 (2005): 3.

9. Keith C. Barton, "Historical Sources in the Classroom: Purpose and Use," *HSSE online* 7, no. 2 (2018): 10.

10. Jearl Nix and C. H. Bohan, "Looking at the Past for Help in the Present: The Role of Historical Photos in Middle and Secondary History Classes," *Ohio Social Studies Review* 51, no. 2 (2014): 15.

11. For a comprehensive guide to using artwork, see Ludmilla Jordanova, *The Look of the Past: Visual and Material Evidence in Historical Practice* (Cambridge: Cambridge University Press, 2012).

12. Judy Reinhartz and Dennis Reinhartz, "'How Wide the World': Geography, Maps, and the Teaching of American History," *OAH Magazine of History* 7, no. 3 (1993): 22, 26.

13. Steven S. Volk, "How to Navigate an 'Upside-Down' World: Using Images in the History Classroom," *New Directions for Teaching & Learning* 2015, no. 141 (Spring 2015): 63.

14. Cheryl Mason Bolick, "Teaching and Learning with Online Historical Maps," *Social Education* 70, no. 3 (2006): 133. For further discussion on using maps in social studies classrooms see Steven Jennings, "Questions to Facilitate the Use of Maps as Primary Sources in the Classroom," *The Social Studies* 104, no. 5 (2013): 201–6; Mark Newman and Jack Zevin, *Geography as Inquiry: Teaching About and Exploring the Earth as Our Home* (New York: Rowman & Littlefield, 2016); Cristian Parellada and Mario Carretero, "Digital Historical Maps in Classrooms. Challenges in History Education," in *History Education in the Digital Age*, ed. Mario Carretero, María Cantabrana, and Cristian Parellada (Cham, Switzerland: Springer 2022), 139–61.

15. Helen J. Chatterjee, "Object-Based Learning in Higher Education: The Pedagogical Power of Museums," *University Museums and Collections Journal* 3 (2010): 181. For more on using physical objects see Helen J. Chatterjee and Leonie Hannan, *Engaging the Senses: Object-Based Learning in Higher Education* (London: Routledge, 2016); Linda Farr Darling, "Using Artifacts to Foster Historical Inquiry," in *The Anthology of Social Studies: Issues and Strategies for Elementary Teachers*, ed. Roland Case and Penney Clark (Vancouver, BC: Pacific Educational Press, 2008), 283–89.

16. The literature on using images in the classroom is robust and extensive. See Robert Blackey, "To Illuminate History: Making History Picture-Perfect," *Teaching*

History: A Journal of Methods 30, no. 2 (2005): 59–72; Joseph Coohill, "Images and the History Lecture: Teaching the History Channel Generation," *The History Teacher* 39, no. 4 (2006): 455–65; William Gaudelli, "Interpreting Democratic Images: Secondary Students' Reading of Visual Texts," *Teacher Education Quarterly* 36, no. 1 (2009): 111–30; James H. Madison, "Teaching with Images," *OAH Magazine of History* 18, no. 2 (2004): 65–68; Barbara Ormond, "Enabling Students to Read Historical Images: The Value of the Three-Level Guide for Historical Inquiry," *The History Teacher* 44, no. 2 (2011): 179–90; Marjaana Puurtinen, Markus Nivala, and Arja Virta, "Visual Sources and Historical Thinking in Higher Education," *Nordidactica: Journal of Humanities and Social Science Education* 2015, no. 4 (2015): 1–20; Yonghee Suh, "Past Looking: Using Arts as Historical Evidence in Teaching History," *Social Studies Research and Practice* 8, no. 1 (2013), 135–59; Walter Werner, "Reading Visual Texts," *Theory and Research in Social Education* 30, no. 2 (2002): 401–28.

17. Nix and Bohan, "Looking at the Past," 18. Many scholars employ some version of the approach outlined by Jearl Nix and C. H. Bohan to guide students in analyzing photographs. They organize the strategy into three "Looks": "The First Look section consists of observational questions that require students to record what they see in the picture. The Second Look section asks students to respond to questions that challenge them to consider source and context. The Third Look section asks students to infer about the content of the photograph and ask questions of the image." See also, Schocker, "A Case for Using Images," 426.

18. For example, see the British Museum, "Explore the Collection," accessed June 23, 2023, https://www.britishmuseum.org/collection.

19. Library of Congress, "Dorothea Lange's 'Migrant Mother' Photographs in the Farm Security Administration Collection," accessed June 20, 2023, https://guides.loc.gov/migrant-mother/images.

20. *Junior Normal Class of Fisk University, Nashville, Tennessee, Seated on Steps Outside of Building*, n.d. [between 1890 and 1906], photograph, Nashville, TN, Library of Congress Prints and Photographs Division, https://www.loc.gov/item/94513859/.

21. Images of objects are special cases and excluded from this discussion.

22. Warren K. Leffler, *Civil Rights March on Washington, D.C.*, 1963, photograph, Washington, DC, Library of Congress Prints and Photographs Division, https://lccn.loc.gov/2003654393.

23. J. Prockter, *A Correct Map of the World Drawn from the Best Discoveries*, 1760?, map, [London?: Publisher not identified], Library of Congress Geography and Map Division, https://www.loc.gov/item/2017585774/.

24. August R. Ohman, *Missionary Map of the World Showing Prevailing Religions of Its Various Nations and the Central Stations of All Protestant Missionary Societies*, n.d. [1902?], map, New York, Library of Congress Geography and Map Division, https://www.loc.gov/item/2017586281/.

25. Elliot Aronson, The Jigsaw Classroom, Social Psychology Network, accessed June 21, 2023, https://www.jigsaw.org.

26. Some ideas for this activity are based on Nicholas W. Proctor, "Making History: The Breakup Microgame," Reacting Consortium, accessed June 21, 2023, https:

//reactingconsortium.org/games/makinghistory; and Jack Zevin and David Gerwin, *Teaching World History as Mystery* (New York: Routledge, 2011).

27. Two examples are Smithsonian Institution, Smithsonian Learning Lab, accessed June 23, 2023, https://learninglab.si.edu/; and Google Arts & Culture, which uses the Google Sites tool to create websites that are easy for students to create as well. Google Arts & Culture, accessed June 23, 2023, https://artsandculture.google.com/.

28. National Archives, "Mapping History," accessed June 29, 2023, https://www.docsteach.org/tools/mapping-history; Google Earth, "Education," accessed June 29, 2003, https://www.google.com/earth/education/. Google Earth's creation tool provides resources to create mapping projects.

Chapter 6

Role-Playing Games and Simulations

"I transformed into Lonnie King, a co-chair of COAHR (Committee on Appeal for Human Rights) and activist to desegregate Atlanta. I felt Lonnie's pains and I felt as though I said what he would have said. It was as though I was Lonnie, trying to fight for what is just and right regarding African American people in Atlanta. The game provided a gateway that I was able to step into to feel Lonnie's pain, frustrations, and his fear of what could happen to the people that follow his cause."[1] This reflection, written by a young woman in 2022, is one of thousands of similar reflections written by students who participate in Reacting to the Past (RTTP) role-playing games. This pedagogy began in one classroom in the 1990s but has since expanded to hundreds of classrooms and engaged thousands of students. It continues to grow.

The wide-ranging benefits of Reacting to the Past in particular, and other role-playing simulations in general, have been well-documented. Inquiry into the pedagogy continues to develop as a Scholarship of Teaching and Learning research field.[2] This chapter briefly summarizes the pedagogy, discusses some of the most important benefits for the future of history teaching, and then demonstrates how a Reacting mindset can condition instructors to seek action and interaction in a variety of classroom strategies, not limited to full, formal Reacting to the Past games.

IN THEORY

The Reacting Consortium website succinctly summarizes Reacting to the Past in this way:

> In Reacting games, students are assigned character roles with specific goals and must communicate, collaborate, and compete effectively to advance their

objectives. While students are obliged to adhere to the philosophical and intellectual beliefs of the figures they have been assigned to play, as well as the context and facts of the historical moment, they must devise their own means of expressing those ideas persuasively in papers, speeches, or other public presentations. Students must pursue a course of action to try to win the "game."[3]

Reacting has elements of Model United Nations, live action role play (LARP), mock trial, debate, and strategy games all centered on close readings of primary sources. Reacting games put students in the middle of complex decisions in history, and the games unfold according to how the characters interact and how convincing the students are in their roles. The outcomes of games do not necessarily mirror the historical outcomes, yet—crucially—in debriefing sessions after the game, the real historical outcomes are discussed and evaluated against how events proceeded in the game.

Scholarly research on RTTP has examined many facets of the pedagogy, from its usefulness for retention to its long-term effects to its value for student learning.[4] RTTP fits squarely into the requisite characteristics of a "high-impact practice."[5] George D. Kuh lists a number of strategies that are high-impact practices; RTTP fits most fully into "collaborative assignments and projects" and "diversity/global learning." At its best, RTTP integrates almost every element of the "NSSE [National Survey of Student Engagement] Deep/Integrative Learning Scale" from "integrating ideas or information from various sources" to "making judgements about the value of information" to "learning something that changed how you understand an issue."[6]

Running an RTTP module is a significant investment of class time and instructor and student effort. Why not simply hold an in-class debate that engages primary sources and takes less time and work? Do the benefits of RTTP offer a significant return on investment that cannot be achieved other ways?[7]

Part of what makes RTTP distinctive—and a key characteristic that determines its status as a "high impact practice"—is that it is immersive. The time and effort are part of the point of the exercise; the investment in the game creates a world that takes on an identity of its own as students exercise greater control in character. One of the difficulties of an in-class debate or a mock trial is that students can too easily focus on the grade or pleasing the instructor or just doing enough to get the assignment over with. In RTTP, the instructor recedes to the background as students become immersed in the game, and the burden of representing the character accurately provides a unique challenge to each student.

The emotional connection to the characters is a key component of Reacting's "secret sauce." While an in-class debate focuses on the positions to be argued, Reacting focuses on the life stories that bring the issues into conflict. This approach generates much more empathy than debates that are disconnected from real life and historical context. Debating whether young American civil rights activists in 1960 should defer to the staid strategies of their elders is very different from embodying the life story of Lonnie King, leading protests, and arguing over strategy with Atlanta civil rights leaders who, in turn, are feeling pressure from Atlanta politicians (as alluded to in the quote that opens this chapter). The debate is forgettable; being Lonnie King is not.

Another aspect of Reacting that sets it apart from other types of classroom debates and simulations is the use of "indeterminates." These are fully fleshed out historical characters who are missing one thing: a decided opinion on the game's topic. Whether it is considering the design of the Vietnam Memorial or if the Cherokees can be removed from Georgia or if the silk workers of Patterson, New Jersey, should form a union, indeterminates are ready to be persuaded. All efforts of the factions (i.e., established positions) are focused on convincing the indeterminates to join their cause. The need to present convincing arguments—where success or failure in the game is at stake—harnesses students' competitiveness to motivate them to engage with the game.

Whereas an in-class debate might rely on the instructor to act as judge or declare a winner or even use nondebating students as a jury, Reacting raises the stakes by providing in-game incentives for characters to argue convincingly and by providing each student with a well-developed character to represent. Developing the emotional connection to the characters and keeping the focus not on shouting back and forth endlessly but instead pursuing the votes of the indeterminates creates a powerful, immersive experience that can accomplish many learning goals simultaneously.

Even for instructors who recognize the potency of RTTP, the skill required to successfully run a game that keeps all students active and demonstrably accomplishes learning goals might give even the most enthusiastic teachers pause. It is certainly true that RTTP is an advanced pedagogy, and games cannot realize all of their potential if instructors are looking over the materials the night before the game starts. As with any piece of complex equipment, skill, practice, and training are essential for success.

Fortunately, there are many different types of games—and more being developed all the time—with some that are more accessible to new instructors. Some games are simpler to run than others. The Reacting community provides guidance for new instructors who might not feel ready to take on a more advanced game. From conferences to sample games using video conferencing to real-time support through social media, instructors can find all the tools they need to learn how to run successful games, practice with colleagues before using games in the classroom, and troubleshoot specific problems within games.⁸

Because Reacting has so much potential for powerful, deep learning, it is useful for instructors to cultivate a "Reacting mindset" over the course of the semester—long before the game is introduced and even after the game is complete. A Reacting mindset is not simply for students; instructors who filter course content through the lens of Reacting will set themselves and their students up for a successful, immersive learning experience. In addition, instructors may find that a Reacting mindset starts to shape their approach even in courses where no games are used. This chapter outlines a way of thinking for instructors who may not be ready to use RTTP but want to be more intentional about course design and achieving learning goals.

A Reacting Mindset

There are several ways in which approaching a course with a Reacting mindset, no matter what kind of game is used, will lead to better outcomes for students and instructors. This mindset includes fostering deep reading, arguing from evidence, and making decisions. Considering each one in turn will help to elicit more intentionality in course design and delivery, whether or not a game is included.

The foundation of any RTTP game is deep engagement with primary sources. For many instructors, the promise of real engagement with historical text is the whole reason to play the game. While some students will recognize the potency of grounding their character and arguments in the primary sources, Reacting is not a silver bullet that will magically transform a weak reader into a deep reader—although there are plenty of instances where that does occur!

To set up all students to engage deeply with the primary sources, the skills of primary source analysis need to be embedded in the course from day one. Whether through history labs, You Decide lectures, homework assignments, or other analysis practice, all students need frequent exposure to many different types of sources so that they are ready to engage with the game's sources. Savvy instructors will incorporate the types of sources included in the game in earlier assignments. For example, the Flashpoints game about John Brown includes both newspaper articles and speeches. Exposing students to both types of documents and the differences between them—long before John Brown is mentioned—allows students to more quickly analyze the game documents.

Teaching students to recognize the importance of audience is also a necessary skill for using documents effectively in games. Having students practice deciphering the intended and unintended audiences of a document and how the meaning and use of the document might change based on who is reading it allows students to recognize how a document that seems to support one idea could also be used to attack that idea. With that skill, students are equipped to mine all of the documents included in the game book, not just the ones that support their character's stance.

Another component of a Reacting mindset is training students to marshal evidence to make an argument, regardless of personal opinion. For students to move from making an argument without evidence to making an argument grounded entirely in the documents, they need practice making arguments with which they disagree. When students are in character as part of a game, they are reading texts from their character's point of view and interpreting the sources based on the character's life and beliefs. Even if the students personally disagree with the conclusions, they learn how the character *could* hold those beliefs. This skill is a more nuanced way of reading sources and making arguments, rather than picking quotes that support a predetermined idea.[9] An instructor who wants students to make the most of the game will emphasize argument, evidence, and understanding the author's worldview and perspective. Students will then be set up to read the sources from their character's point of view and make arguments that seem logical to their character.

A Reacting mindset can also guide students toward recognizing how individuals made decisions historically. Rather than presenting a flat narrative where all the issues are settled, an instructor with a Reacting mindset might emphasize the process by which historical actors made decisions. For example, showing an election map is an efficient way to show the results of an election, but it removes the excitement and interest of the participants as well as why anyone should care about the results. Similarly, showing the final design of the Vietnam Memorial is very different from exploring the debates about the design. A Reacting mindset helps instructors seek out the decision moments and explore the positions of all involved factions.

IN PRACTICE

This section explores how to use Reacting to the Past games as well as how to use "Reacting-adjacent" simulations and assignments. There are two main types of RTTP games: full-length games and Flashpoints games. Full-length games take two or three weeks or more to play (anywhere from five to fourteen sessions); Flashpoints games take about a week (two to three sessions). There are pros and cons for each type.

Full-length games offer a truly immersive experience. The role sheets are extensive, and students have time to fully understand their characters. The game unfolds dramatically as events and decisions build on one another.

Among the benefits of a full-length game is that even the most reluctant or confused student will eventually get involved as the game continues class after class. In addition, a longer game allows students to fully engage with the sources—to use them in their writing assignments and speeches and to repeatedly engage with them to persuade the indeterminates.

One of the most commonly repeated objections to a full-length game is the time investment, particularly in a survey course.[10] Two or three weeks of class time plus the setup sessions is the length of a whole unit. RTTP instructors argue that trading "coverage" for depth is worth it, especially when coverage would otherwise be happening through content-heavy lectures that most students do not fully pay attention to.[11] Further, survey instructors can choose games on topics that they would like students to understand more deeply. For example, spending three weeks exploring the French Revolution or the Constitutional Convention is efficacious if the payoff is deep learning about such foundational events.

Nevertheless, content concerns or the attention span of lower-level students might prompt instructors to use a Flashpoints game instead. These shorter games narrow the scope of the issues or events presented in the game, without sacrificing character development or engagement with primary sources. Flashpoints games use fewer primary sources and focus on one or two moments of conflict within a historical event. Rather than looking at a whole range of debates about the U.S. Constitution, for example, the *Raising the Eleventh Pillar* Flashpoints game focuses only on the New York State Ratifying Convention in 1788.[12]

The disadvantage of a Flashpoints game is that it happens quickly. Students who are confused or not prepared for the first session might not become active until the game is almost over. It is all the more important, therefore, for instructors to have a Reacting mindset from the first day of the semester. If instructors are guiding students on how to analyze documents, make arguments from evidence, and recognize how decisions are made, students will be equipped to jump into the game and succeed. An instructor who lectures all semester and then drops in a Flashpoint game may be disappointed at the outcome, and students may be frustrated by the requirements. By contrast, a Reacting-minded instructor will prepare their students and then deploy the game as the culmination of the students' practice, resulting in a much better chance of achieving learning goals.

RTTP games offer a wide range of benefits, and it is up to the instructor to choose which ones will best support or achieve student learning objectives. For example, if one of the course goals is for students to effectively analyze and use primary source evidence, the instructor can more heavily weight the written assignments and award points for using primary source evidence accurately during game sessions. Contrastingly, if the learning goal is to build a learning community among the class, instructors can emphasize how engaged game play helps everyone learn more and can award points accordingly. In both instances—and others that are easily imagined—the instructor must recognize that RTTP games are not panaceas, and it is the instructor's responsibility to set students up for success.

Both full-length and Flashpoints games use the essential elements of RTTP: role sheets, indeterminates, victory objectives, core texts, and debriefs. Understanding the importance of these elements not only helps Reacting-minded instructors position students to fulfill learning objectives; it can also spark creation of Reacting-adjacent assignments that benefit from using the essential elements.

Considering the first element, each character in the game has a role sheet which grounds the character in historical reality. Almost all Reacting characters are depictions of real historical figures or amalgamations of several historical figures to create a type, such as a "Pennsylvania landowner" or a "Vietnam veteran who supported the war." Critically, role sheets describe the character in second person, using "you" to tell the character's biography, as in "You are John Brown, instigator of the raid on Harper's Ferry."[13] Using second person pushes the reader into the story and into thinking from the character's point of view.[14] Role sheets also include such pertinent information as potential allies and enemies, special powers or responsibilities, and relationships to the main ideas.

Some characters are indeterminates (described above). Indeterminates are critical to the game's success and a key marker of difference between RTTP games and in-class debates. These characters have personal histories and goals, but they are open to be persuaded regarding the main topic of the game. Indeterminates are such a powerful part of the game because they provide real-world evidence of the importance of choices and decisions. As crafty as the individual factions might be, the game hinges on their ability to convince indeterminates to join their side.

As an illustration of the importance of indeterminates, this student reflection shows a level of engagement that went beyond mere winning and losing: "Overall, I think that we were pretty successful (we did end up getting the most votes on the last day), but I will say that I had wished for a more complete victory. Or at the least, I felt that we could have persuaded more of the [indeterminates] to vote for our cause."[15] The student recognized why indeterminates are particularly potent—they provide an effective barometer of the argument's persuasiveness.

Next, victory objectives guide the game and provide direction to each player's decisions and actions. This element distinguishes a game from an in-class debate because they go beyond merely winning the final vote or judgment. Victory objectives include specific actions players should take that are key to the game's success. One player's goals might instruct them to form a splinter movement; another's might encourage them to raise specific objections to an opponent's plan; another's might lead a character to raise or spend in-game money to support a cause. Most vibrantly, victory objectives give each player specific work to do during each game session, and therefore, winning hinges on being active and engaged.

The integration of the core texts, or primary source readings, into the role sheets and the victory objectives keeps the game centered on the documents. While there is a temptation to let the game elements supersede the discussion and understanding of texts, a well-crafted game interweaves the key ideas and the texts into all elements of game play. Instructors can reinforce the importance of documents at several steps along the way: giving students enough time and scaffolding to read the texts before the game begins, thoroughly explaining how students should use texts in their written work and speeches and giving in-game or out-of-game rewards (i.e., course participation points) to students who effectively use the documents over the course of the game.

At its heart, Reacting games are about activating the "protégé effect" or the benefits that come from learning something in order to teach it to someone else.[16] Unlike a presentation, which elicits little response other than polite applause, an in-game speech instructs the audience while also generating engaged discussion, particularly because victory objectives are on the line.

These essential elements—role sheets, indeterminates, victory objectives, and core texts—are present in both full-length and Flashpoints games, and students will meet learning objectives most effectively when instructors are working to highlight and activate all four elements. One further element is present most fully in full-length games but is also important to Flashpoints and a useful exercise for many Reacting-adjacent strategies: the debrief.

At the end of the game, the instructor moves back into a leadership position and guides students through exercises to reflect on what happened in the game, how it compares to what happened historically, why there are similarities and differences, and how students can think metacognitively about the experience. This debrief time has many benefits. Even if the game ended differently from the historical outcome, students are primed to think about the reasons for the historical outcome and the role of individuals in creating the historical outcome.

The debrief is also the time for students to step out of their role and think about their thought processes while in character. This can be done through small and large group discussion. A reflection assignment as the final assignment of the game also allows students to evaluate their thinking and actions in the game as well as how they responded to the conclusion, both emotionally and intellectually.[17]

The debrief is critically important to closing the loop in a game-based learning experience. A debrief or reflection will be most effective, however, if the instructor has employed a Reacting mindset throughout the course. Introducing metacognitive assignments for the first time at the end of the game is not as fruitful as introducing them earlier in the semester and assigning several opportunities to practice. Then, when the game ends, students are not learning a new skill but instead fully benefiting from a skill they have been practicing by applying it in a new context.

Reacting and In-Class Debates

Some courses do not lend themselves well to gameplay, and some teachers cannot afford the class time to play a game. Nevertheless, the main elements of Reacting can be adapted to enhance in-class debates that might span just one or two class periods. Debate is a common active learning strategy, whether it is highly structured or informal.[18] Giving students a position to defend (or letting them choose), allowing them to research the position, and then engaging them in debate to defend their position and attack the opposite position can be adapted to many lessons and issues in history classes. Debates also function as real-world simulations, mimicking the debates that historical actors joined in the past.[19]

Sometimes, however, classroom debates do not live up to their potential. Students may be lackluster in defending an assigned position or a position with which they do not personally agree. Some students do not respond well to the confrontational nature of a debate, or it is too easy for a few students to dominate the discussion. Studies show that only two to six students actively participate in an in-class debate, with everyone else content to watch or disengage. In addition, a debate can unintentionally teach that a given issue only has two sides, with no option to compromise. While competition can be a fun way to spark student engagement, the competitive nature of debate can cause students to disengage if they feel that they are on the losing side.[20]

A Reacting-informed debate activity can address many of these pitfalls. Rather than having the instructor or the nondebating students acting as judges, using the idea of indeterminates can add more depth and urgency to the debate. For example, if two sides are debating the merits of expanding the electorate to include women, giving the nondebaters short role sheets that assign them the characteristics of a person who might have heard these debates historically can keep them engaged.

Assigning several types of roles—for example, an older male politician, a young working woman, an older married mother, an eighteen-year-old male immigrant—ensures that the audience will be persuaded by the arguments in different ways. In that scenario, the side in favor of expanding the electorate is not the obvious winning side as a portion of the listeners are already biased against them. This strategy—perhaps pared with a reflection assignment—keeps all students actively attentive and teaches more layers of history than debating in a modern context otherwise would.

Another way that a Reacting mindset can enhance classroom debate is to use the concept of victory objectives to expand the debate beyond winning and losing. If debate tends to accentuate binary outcomes which are often ahistorical, then victory objectives provide space for a range of outcomes.[21] To continue the example of a debate about expanding the electorate, rather than only having a simple win or lose result, victory objectives provide a range from total victory to partial victory to compromise to defeat. As debaters quickly argue themselves into a position where total victory is unattainable, they can move toward a partial victory or compromise. This transforms the exercise from a debate into a negotiation, allowing for a greater depth of historical complexity and more agency for the debaters.

Reacting-inspired debates can also set up deeper metacognition in the reflection phase of the assignment. While it is common practice for instructors to assign audience members to write a reflection explaining who they thought won the debate and why, audience members playing the roles of indeterminates can judge the debate in character and then step out of their role and reflect on why the debate persuaded their character, even if their real selves would not have been persuaded.[22]

Similarly, debaters working with a range of victory objectives can reflect on their choices and compare those choices to what happened historically, as well as their personal stance on the issue. Thinking about the debate and the outcome from a variety of perspectives, therefore, increases the learning benefits of the assignment. In addition, a deeper and more memorable experience is easier to refer back to throughout the rest of the course, which makes the time investment all the more worthwhile.

Reacting-Inspired Assignments

A Reacting mindset corresponds most directly to classroom debates, but assignments that are further afield can also benefit from Reacting's strengths. Reading primary sources from a historical perspective is a key building block in any history course, but it can be difficult to teach students to abandon their present, personal perspective and read documents from the point of view of their historical audience. In a Reacting game, however, the primary sources seem to jump off the page as students become immersed in their characters.

While it will not bring all of the benefits of a game, giving students short character role sheets before reading major documents or sets of sources can deepen student understanding of both the text and the historical context. If the instructor distributes several types of characters, the benefits extend even farther as students learn, through discussion, that documents are interpreted quite differently based on the reader's perspective. If there is a whole set of documents to analyze, the lesson can consist of reading, discussing, and writing about the documents from the point of view of multiple historical figures, whether those figures are real people or a composite type.

For example, assigning students to read excerpts from Fanny Kemble's *Journal of a Residence on a Georgia Plantation* (1863) can be an illuminating look at plantation life and the influences of abolitionism in the United States. Modern readers are automatically sympathetic to Kemble's perspective and those of the enslaved people on the plantation. That sympathy, however, does not help students fully understand how the slave system in the United States lasted as long as it did or why people were willing to die for it in the Civil War.

To teach students to read the document from a historical perspective, therefore, the instructor can hand out one-paragraph role sheets to each student. Some students are Fanny Kemble herself, reading over her newly published book. Others are her ex-husband Pierce Butler, reflecting on his status as a member of one of the most prominent Southern families but also reeling from the recent debt-induced sale (1859) of most of the people he had kept in slavery. Others are the intended audience of British people who are undecided on whether they should support the Confederacy or not. Still others could be free black abolitionists in Philadelphia.[23]

Each person or composite character will notice different aspects of the document and interpret it differently. The instructor can then lead the class in recognizing and understanding the value of seeing a document from a variety of perspectives and using those differences to generate new avenues of inquiry. Therefore, what might have been a sleepy read-through of a historical text comes alive by harnessing a Reacting mindset and helps students develop historical thinking.

Reacting-Inspired Research Papers

For students in introductory or survey history classes, a Reacting-inspired research paper can help them understand primary sources more deeply, as well as the necessity of using primary source evidence to craft an effective argument. Rather than assigning students to write a standard research paper from the point of view of the objective present, instructors can take inspiration from the written assignments in Reacting games. Both traditional research papers and Reacting writing assignments have persuasion as one of their main purposes, but when students are writing from the point of view of a character trying to persuade indeterminates, the assignment *feels* more purposeful and thus taps into student's emotions to provide motivation and interest in completing the assignment well.

This shift can be seen in an example of a Reacting inspired paper prompt about the 1911 Triangle Shirtwaist Factory fire in New York City:

> It is December 1912. You are a progressive reformer writing an essay about the Triangle Factory fire for publication in a national magazine. Choose either gender, working conditions, or the garment industry as the focus for your essay and answer the following question: *What reforms regarding gender, working conditions, or the garment industry need to be made to ensure the Triangle Factory disaster never happens again?*
>
> Paper requirements:
>
> 1. Choose one area of reform to focus on. Build your argument around your proposed reform. Consider possible objections to your reform, based on the history and the documents.
> 2. Discuss in depth a minimum of two documents from Jo Ann E. Argersinger, *The Triangle Fire: A Brief History with Documents*. An in-depth discussion includes all of the relevant facts and information about the document (Who wrote it? When? Why? Who read it? What is the historical context? How does it fit into the rest of the story? What biases are present? Etc.) and uses the document to support your position. Use quotes sparingly and only when the particular phrasing is necessary for your point.[24]

The instructor provides the point of view and the audience and gives the student a choice about the focus of the essay. The documents—which students are otherwise often tempted to only cursorily reference—are integral to proving the necessity of reform. This Reacting-inspired paper prompt offers instructors a useful way to introduce students to the basics of research papers, which the instructor can also link to other Reacting-inspired assignments throughout the semester. Instructors can repeatedly replicate this type of assignment for papers where there is a designated set of sources or when students must find their own set of sources. It also works for papers where the learning goal is to demonstrate the importance of evidence-based arguments.

CUSTOMIZE

Reacting to the Past has spread through so many high school and college classrooms because of the brilliance of its central premise and its adaptability to a wide variety of courses and instructors. Through practice and experience, instructors figure out what scaffolding or additional complexities are necessary to make the games successful for their students. Teachers also recognize how employing a Reacting mindset all semester can make the games more effective in achieving learning goals and spread the benefits of the methodology beyond the game itself.

Aside from the differences between Flashpoints games and full-length games, there are other ways for instructors to make the games their own. Many Reacting instructors have successfully adapted games to be played fully online. Others might start the first one to two sessions of the game and then pause to provide additional scaffolding instruction for students—whether through document analysis, paper development, or historical context. Other instructors use a game in class and then challenge their students to work together to write a game about a different topic. Teachers can further adapt this idea by assigning students to write only the role sheets about an imagined game and to find the supporting primary sources to help that character succeed.[25]

After running a few games, many instructors are inspired to write their own games to match the particular needs of their classes. While there are many resources available to write a full game, many games start as single-day lessons with short role sheets, readings, and simple victory objectives and then grow from there.[26] Keeping in mind the simple formula of having more indeterminates than members of any one faction ensures that the game will "work"—that is, the factions cannot simply call for a vote and win based on sheer numbers; they have to do the work of arguing to convince indeterminates. From there, the game writer can add in as many game elements, special powers, or secret objectives as they wish. Running the game once will spark new ideas to make it more interactive and complex.[27]

As previously stated, a Reacting mindset can even be employed in classes where no games are used. For any class with a summative assessment, the instructor can use backward course design to ensure that students are as prepared to perform as they would need to be in a game. While a game uses positive social pressure (i.e., the desire to work together as a team to win) to motivate students to prepare and participate, instructors in non-Reacting classes can think through—and even share with students—what the victory objectives are regarding each summative assessment. Setting up students to succeed is the heart of the instructor's role in running a game, and it can be applied even in non-Reacting settings.

CONCLUSION

Reacting to the Past games are a high-impact educational practice that immerse students in historical events and ideas. They allow students to drive their own learning and motivate each other. In order for the games to realize their full potential, instructors must be preparing students to take full advantage of the learning opportunity the games provide. By practicing deep reading, perspective taking, making evidence-based arguments, and other historical thinking strategies, instructors provide students with the skills they need to succeed in both the game and in their continued study of history.

Whether instructors decide to use a game or other role-play simulation or not, a Reacting mindset can bring the benefits of this high-impact practice into many different types of courses. Keeping in mind the essential elements of Reacting—role sheets, victory objectives, indeterminates, core texts, and debriefing—can transform many lackluster activities and assignments into engaging experiences. Using these elements to foster historical thinking will benefit students and energize the teacher.

Reacting to the Past games and other simulations are popular because they are effective. Nevertheless, the pedagogy is not going to appeal to every instructor. Choosing not to run a game does not mean forsaking the benefits of a Reacting-inspired mindset, for both teachers and students. In fact, the content and skills required to complete a game successfully also fulfill learning goals related to historical thinking. The essence of RTTP is an active and interactive strategy to engage all learners, read texts deeply, and see events from a variety of perspectives, whether experienced through a game or through a Reacting-inspired assignment.

NOTES

1. The student was playing the role of Lonnie King in Robert Baker, Marni Davis, Curtis Jackson, Jared Poley, and Jeffrey Young, "The Atlanta Sit-Ins: A Reacting to the Past Game in Development," (unpublished).

2. Mark Carnes, *Minds on Fire: How Role-Immersion Games Transform College* (Cambridge, MA: Harvard University Press, 2018). Additional essays and peer-reviewed research are compiled on the Reacting Consortium website, see "Book / Essay / Article Bibliography," accessed July 12, 2023, https://reactingconsortium.org/bibliography.

3. Reacting Consortium, "What Is Reacting," accessed October 18, 2022. https://reactingconsortium.org/WIR-basics.

4. The best way to become acquainted with Reacting to the Past is to play a game. The second-best way is to explore the website, reactingconsortium.org. Scholarship on the effectiveness of Reacting in a variety of areas is best summarized in C. Edward Watson and Thomas Chase Hagood, eds., *Playing to Learn with Reacting to the Past: Research on High Impact, Active Learning Practices* (Cham, Switzerland: Palgrave Macmillan, 2018).

5. For a sample of articles that make this claim: José Bowen, "Reacting to the Past Will Revive your Teaching," *Teaching Naked Blog*, July 15, 2016, https:

//teachingnaked.com/reacting-to-the-past-with-revive-your-teaching/; Colleen Flaherty, "Scaling Up High-Impact Instruction," *Inside Higher Ed*, September 27, 2016, https://www.insidehighered.com/news/2016/09/28/new-grants-help-institutions-embed-reacting-past-other-high-impact-teaching; Russell Olwell and Azibo Stevens, "'I Had to Double Check My Thoughts': How the Reacting to the Past Methodology Impacts First-Year College Student Engagement, Retention, and Historical Thinking," *The History Teacher* 48, no. 3 (May 2015): 561–72.

    6. George D. Kuh, "High-Impact Educational Practices: What They Are, Who Has Access to Them, and Why They Matter" (Washington, DC: Association of American Colleges and Universities, 2008), 9–10, 23, accessed July 12, 2023, https://provost.tufts.edu/celt/files/High-Impact-Ed-Practices1.pdf.

    7. The benefits of in-class debate are well-documented, and RTTP takes advantage of many of them while also avoiding common pitfalls. For an introduction to some of the benefits of classroom debate see Karyl A. Davis, M. Leslie Wade Zorwick, James Roland, and Melissa Maxcy Wade, eds., *Using Debate in the Classroom: Encouraging Critical Thinking, Communication, and Collaboration* (New York: Routledge, 2016); Ruth Kennedy, "In-Class Debates: Fertile Ground for Active Learning and the Cultivation of Critical Thinking and Oral Communication Skills," *International Journal of Teaching and Learning in Higher Education* 19, no. 2 (2007): 187–90; Pezhman Zare and Moomala Othman, "Classroom Debate as a Systematic Teaching/Learning Approach," *World Applied Sciences Journal* 28, no. 11 (2013): 1506–13.

    8. Reacting Consortium, Reacting Faculty Lounge, Facebook group page (private), accessed July 12, 2023, https://www.facebook.com/groups/reactingfacultylounge.

    9. Olwell and Stevens, "I Had to Double Check My Thoughts," 567–68.

    10. For a discussion of many of the pros and cons, see Michael LaCombe, "Teaching with Games Roundtable Q&A—Michael LaCombe with the Authors," University of Pennsylvania, *Early American Studies Miscellany*, July 15, 2022, https://web.sas.upenn.edu/earlyamericanstudies/2022/07/15/teaching-with-games-roundtable-qa/.

    11. James M. Lang, "Stop Blaming Students for Your Listless Classroom," *The Chronicle of Higher Education*, September 29, 2014, https://www.chronicle.com/article/stop-blaming-students-for-your-listless-classroom/.

    12. John Patrick Coby, *Raising the Eleventh Pillar: The Ratification Debate of 1788* (New York: W.W. Norton and Company, 2021).

    13. These are illustrative examples, not exact quotes, drawn from the following games: M. Rebecca Livingstone, Kelly McFall, and Abigail Perkiss, *Monuments and Memory-Making: The Debate over the Vietnam Veterans Memorial, 1981–1982* (Chapel Hill: University of North Carolina Press, 2023); Bill Offutt, *The Fate of John Brown, 1859*, accessed July 12, 2023, https://reactingconsortium.org/games/johnbrown1859; Nicholas W. Proctor, *Forest Diplomacy: Cultures in Conflict on the Pennsylvania Frontier, 1757* (Chapel Hill: University of North Carolina Press, 2022).

    14. In some ways, role sheets derive from the educational strategy of using case studies, in that role sheets present a story, an emotional connection, and a complex problem to solve (i.e., the victory objectives). See Barbara Gross Davis, "Case Studies," in *Tools for Teaching*, 2nd ed. (San Francisco: Jossey-Bass, 2009), 222–29.

15. The student was playing Elizabeth George, "'Am I Not a Woman and a Sister?' Anti-Slavery and Women's Rights: A Reacting to the Past Game in Development," (unpublished)

16. Catherine Chase, Doris Chin, Marily Oppezzo, and Daniel Schwartz, "Teachable Agents and the Protégé Effect: Increasing the Effort Towards Learning," *Journal of Science Education & Technology* 18, no. 4 (2009): 354–52.

17. Naomi Silver, "Reflective Pedagogies and the Metacognitive Turn in College Teaching" in *Using Reflection and Metacognition to Improve Student Learning: Across the Disciplines, Across the Academy*, ed. Matthew Kaplan, Naomi Silver, Danielle LaVaque-Manty, and Deborah Meizlish (Sterling, VA: Stylus Publishing, 2013).

18. Pezhman Zare and Moomala Othman, "Students' Perceptions toward Using Classroom Debate to Develop Critical Thinking and Oral Communication Ability," *Asian Social Science* 11, no. 9 (2015): 161.

19. Jeffrey S. Lantis, "Ethics and Foreign Policy: Structured Debates for the International Studies Classroom," *International Studies Perspectives* 5, no. 2 (2004), 122. Structured debates go further by allowing deeper engagement with the material through assigning positions, developing group debate arguments, and participating in a structured format.

20. Ruth Kennedy, "In-Class Debates: Fertile Ground for Active Learning and the Cultivation of Critical Thinking and Oral Communication Skills," *International Journal of Teaching and Learning in Higher Education* 19, no. 2 (2007), 183, 186.

21. Kennedy, "In-Class Debates," 183.

22. Kennedy, "In-Class Debates," 188; Silver, "Reflective Pedagogies," 1–3.

23. John A. Scott, editor's introduction, Fanny Kemble, *Journal of a Residence on a Georgia Plantation in 1838–1839* (Athens: University of Georgia Press, 1984), ix–lxi.

24. The sources for this assignment are from Jo Ann E. Argersinger, *The Triangle Fire: A Brief History with Documents*, 3rd ed. (New York: Bedford / St. Martin's, 2016).

25. Much of the discussion about adapting games to particular classrooms happens on the Reacting Faculty Lounge Facebook page.

26. See Nicholas W. Proctor, *Reacting to the Past Game Designer's Handbook*, 4th ed. (CreateSpace Independent Publishing Platform, 2018).

27. Designers who are ready to take their games to the next level can play test their games at the annual Reacting to the Past Game Design Conference. The Reacting Consortium also provides resources for game authors: "Game Author Resources," Reacting Consortium, accessed July 12, 2023, https://reactingconsortium.org/game-author-resources.

Conclusion

Historians know better than to try to predict the future. One might hypothesize that technology will continue to challenge and change how instructors teach history. Perhaps in-person classrooms with human teachers will be reserved only for those who can afford them, or perhaps technology will foster richer connections and innovations. However the future unfolds, it will still be up to teachers to make the classroom a special place where students can grow and transform.

In the current world, it is not uncommon for college students to enter a classroom and sit quietly looking at their phones. New etiquette norms dictate that it is almost rude to interrupt someone who is even just casually scrolling on their phone, and students are less likely to strike up conversations with the students sitting around them. This behavior does not mean that students do not want to connect with each other and build friendships; often they do. It does mean, however, that teachers will need to work a little harder to create classroom communities where students feel welcome, comfortable, and engaged.

This role for teachers does not mean that the instructor needs to supply all the energy in the room. Rather, creating deep learning experiences where students have opportunities to work together, share ideas, and participate in teams and groups can make use of the abundant student energy in the classroom to create a dynamic learning environment. It may mean that instructors give up some measure of visible control and that progress proceeds at the pace of student learning, not predetermined content coverage goals.

The purpose of this type of active and interactive classroom is not simply for students to find friends and learn from each other. In a history classroom that is guided by the approaches in this book, the goal is for students to be equipped with both historical literacy and historical thinking skills. These strategies should energize students to learn on their own and from each other as well as prepare them to advance to a deeper study of history. By doing history, even at a rudimentary level, students gain a much clearer understanding of history as an informed and changing conversation, rather than a dull parade of names and dates.

This book examined six different methods for developing students' historical thinking skills. The You Decide lecture format allows students to experience the contingencies and choices that historical actors faced. Instructors can cultivate student attention around You Decide moments and "reveal" moments so that students are primed to pay attention to, understand, and remember the historical content. As students discuss and debate their decisions, they see how events of the past were not inevitable any more than the events of their future will be.

History lab assignments mimic the archival process that engages historians by allowing students to "wander" through only slightly curated sets of sources. Students gain content knowledge as they work to develop arguments out of their historical discoveries. Working as a team, students practice historical thinking skills by considering sourcing, context, and interpretation for the documents and using that deeper understanding to answer research questions.

Few activities can shake a classroom out of the doldrums as effectively as games, but for a game to be a worthwhile use of class time, the game must help the instructor teach and reinforce historical thinking. Even when instructors are committed to optimizing board game–based learning, they might be reluctant to take on the burden of running games. With some creative workarounds, however, even nongamer instructors can use board games to teach history.

History teachers are already aware of the power that stories have to grab student attention and convey content knowledge. Nevertheless, teachers can leverage stories even more to act not just as illustrations for lists of facts but rather as the frame through which students examine a portion of the past. By inviting students into the process of crafting stories, instructors help students see the interpretive work that historians do. Students, in turn, learn how much richer their own interpretations of the past can be when they include multiple perspectives and allow for nuance and ambiguity.

As instructors cultivate student attention and give them opportunities to practice deep reading of historical records, developing students' visual literacy can allow them to expand the types of sources they can use. By arming students with the tools to both understand the content, context, and sourcing of images as well as their multifaceted use in answering research questions, instructors show students the value and application of historical thinking skills to varied contexts and sources. Photographs may be the most accessible example, but artwork, maps, and even images of objects all present new and complex views of the past that can enliven students' understanding and engagement.

Complex role-playing games such as Reacting to the Past and other high-impact practices offer the tantalizing promise of immersive, student-led engagement in historical study. These types of activities work best when the instructor approaches the course with a Reacting mindset that works to use many different assignments to prepare students for deep engagement. Readying students with the skills they need to succeed long before the debate or game or mock trial is on the line will ensure that student learning eclipses even the fun and excitement of the activity. This mindset can shape instructors' approaches to learning activities even in courses where a high-impact practice is not used. A Reacting mindset can add depth and urgency even to well-worn learning activities.

For teachers to succeed in this work, they must demonstrate care for students and exercise care for themselves. Mastering the basics—knowing students' names, giving useful and timely feedback, structuring an organized course—creates opportunities to deploy high-impact practices successfully. At the same time, instructors should regulate their workload, particularly by considering to what extent grading time translates into student learning so that they can avoid burnout. Developing one's teaching approach over the span of several years can reduce the preparation workload and allow for refining and reworking specific strategies.

At the same time, teaching real history and providing opportunities for students to do it themselves can be energizing for teachers. Seeing students become immersed in a role-playing game or debate, joining students in asking questions about an image, and eavesdropping as students play out historical decisions in You Decide choices can all be absorbing and engaging for the teacher. Watching students awaken to the thrill of historical study is fulfilling for the teacher and can counteract some of the inevitably repetitive parts of the job.

By engaging the past, not just memorizing a version of it, students experience why historians are passionate about history. This approach serves both students and the discipline well.

Bibliography

Aiken, Katherine. "Superhero History: Using Comic Books to Teach U.S. History." *OAH Magazine of History* 24, no. 2 (2010): 41–47.
American Library Association. "ACRL Visual Literacy Competency Standards for Higher Education." October 27, 2011. https://www.ala.org/acrl/standards/visualliteracy.
———. "Companion Document to the ACRL Framework for Information Literacy for Higher Education." April 6, 2022. https://www.ala.org/acrl/sites/ala.org.acrl/files/content/standards/Framework_Companion_Visual_Literacy.pdf.
Anderson, Fred, and Andrew Cayton. "The Problem of Authority in the Writing of Early American History." *The William and Mary Quarterly* 66, no. 3 (2009): 467–94.
Andrews, Thomas, and Flannery Burke. "What Does It Mean to Think Historically?" *Perspectives on History*, January 1, 2007. https://www.historians.org/research-and-publications/perspectives-on-history/january-2007/what-does-it-mean-to-think-historically.
Apperley, Tom. "Modding the Historians' Code: Historical Verisimilitude and the Counterfactual Imagination." In *Playing with the Past: Digital Games and the Simulation of History*, edited by Matthew Kappell and Andrew Elliot, chap. 12. New York: Bloomsbury Academic, 2013.
Argersinger, Jo Ann E. *The Triangle Fire: A Brief History with Documents*. 3rd ed. New York: Bedford / St. Martins, 2016.
Aronson, Elliot. The Jigsaw Classroom. Social Psychology Network. Accessed June 21, 2023. https://www.jigsaw.org/.
Arum, Richard, Josipa Roksa, and Amanda Cook, eds. *Improving Quality in American Higher Education: Learning Outcomes and Assessments for the 21st Century*. San Francisco: John Wiley & Sons, 2016.
Bage, Grant. *Narrative Matters: Teaching History through Story*. London: Routledge, 1999.
Bain, Ken. *Super Courses: The Future of Teaching and Learning*. Princeton: Princeton University Press, 2021.
Banner, Lois W. "Biography as History." *The American Historical Review* 114, no. 3 (2009): 579–86.

Baron, Christine. "Structuring Historic Site-Based History Laboratories for Teacher Education." *The Journal of Museum Education* 39, no. 1 (2014): 10–19.

Barton, Keith C. "Historical Sources in the Classroom: Purpose and Use." *HSSE online* 7, no. 2 (2018): 1–11.

Begy, Jason. "Board Games and the Construction of Cultural Memory." *Games and Culture* 12, nos. 7–8 (2017): 718–38.

Blackey, Robert. "To Illuminate History: Making History Picture-Perfect." *Teaching History: A Journal of Methods* 30, no. 2 (2005): 59–72.

Blank, Hartmut, and Steffen Nestler. "Perceiving Events as Both Inevitable and Unforeseeable in Hindsight: The Leipzig Candidacy for the Olympics." *British Journal of Social Psychology* 45, no. 1 (2006): 149–60.

Blevins, Cameron. *Paper Trails: The US Post and the Making of the American West.* New York: Oxford University Press, 2021.

———. "Postal Geography and the Golden West" (blog post). October 30, 2014. https://www.cameronblevins.org/posts/postal-geography-and-the-golden-west/.

Bolick, Cheryl Mason. "Teaching and Learning with Online Historical Maps." *Social Education* 70, no. 3 (2006): 133–37.

Borg, Richard. Memoir '44. Los Altos, CA: Days of Wonder, 2004. Board game.

Boston Public Library. "The Liberator (Boston, Mass.: 1831–1865)." Accessed September 9, 2023. https://www.digitalcommonwealth.org/collections/commonwealth:9w032b61n.

Bowen, José. "Reacting to the Past Will Revive Your Teaching." *Teaching Naked Blog.* July 15, 2016. https://josebowen.com/reacting-to-the-past-will-revive-your-teaching/.

Boxleiter, Mike, Tommy Maranges, and Max Temkin. Secret Hitler. Chicago: Goat Wolf & Cabbage, 2016. Board game.

British Museum. "Explore the Collection." Accessed June 23, 2023. https://www.britishmuseum.org/collection.

Brown, Peter C., Henry L. Roediger III, and Mark A. McDaniel, *Making It Stick: The Science of Successful Learning.* Cambridge, MA: Belknap Press, 2014.

Bruff, Derek. Interview with Patrick Rael. *Leading Lines Podcast* (podcast audio). April 18, 2022. https://ir.vanderbilt.edu/handle/1803/17559.

Burke, Alison. "Group Work: How to Use Groups Effectively." *The Journal of Effective Teaching* 11, no. 2 (2011): 87–95.

Burke, Robert. Operation F.A.U.S.T. Robert Burke Games, 2015. Board game.

Calder, Lendol. "The Stories We Tell." *OAH Magazine of History* 27, no. 3 (2013): 5–8. http://www.jstor.org/stable/23489726.

———. "Uncoverage: Toward a Signature Pedagogy for the History Survey." *The Journal of American History* 92, no. 4 (2006): 1358–70. https://doi.org/10.2307/4485896.

Calder, Lendol, and Tracy Steffes. "Measuring College Learning in History." In *Improving Quality in American Higher Education: Learning Outcomes and Assessments for the 21st Century*, edited by Richard Arum, Josipa Roksa, and Amanda Cook, 37–86. San Francisco: John Wiley & Sons, 2016.

Card, Jane. "Picturing Place: What You Get May Be More Than What You See." *Teaching History* 116 (2004).
Carnes, Mark. *Minds on Fire: How Role Immersion Games Transform College.* Cambridge, MA: Harvard University Press, 2014.
Carr, David. *Time, Narrative, and History.* Bloomington: Indiana University Press, 1986.
Cartography Associates. "David Rumsey Map Collection." Accessed September 22, 2022. https://www.davidrumsey.com/home.
Center for Digital Research in the Humanities. "Journals of the Lewis & Clark Expedition." Accessed September 9, 2023. https://lewisandclarkjournals.unl.edu/.
Chapman, Adam. "Privileging Form over Content: Analysing Historical Videogames." *Journal of Digital Humanities* 1, no. 2 (2012): 42–46.
Chase, Catherine, Doris Chin, Marily Oppezzo, and Daniel Schwartz. "Teachable Agents and the Protégé Effect: Increasing the Effort Towards Learning." *Journal of Science Education & Technology* 18, no. 4 (2009): 334–52.
Chatterjee, Helen J. "Object-Based Learning in Higher Education: The Pedagogical Power of Museums." University Museums and Collections Journal 3 (2010).
Chatterjee, Helen J., and Leonie Hannan. *Engaging the Senses: Object-Based Learning in Higher Education.* London: Routledge, 2016.
Chung, Sheng Kuan. "Critical Visual Literacy." *The International Journal of Arts Education* 11, no. 2 (2013): 1–36.
Ciancia, Kathryn, and Edith Sheffer. "Creating Lives: Fictional Characters in the History Classroom." *Perspectives on History*, October 2013. https://www.historians.org/publications-and-directories/perspectives-on-history/october-2013/creating-lives-fictional-characters-in-the-history-classroom.
Coby, John Patrick. *Raising the Eleventh Pillar: The Ratification Debate of 1788.* New York: W.W. Norton and Company, 2021.
Commonplace: The Journal of Early American Life. Accessed June 5, 2023. https://commonplace.online.
Coohill, Joseph. "Images and the History Lecture: Teaching the History Channel Generation." *The History Teacher* 39, no. 4 (2006): 455–65.
Corman, Steven R. "The Difference between Story and Narrative." Center for Strategic Communication. Arizona State University, March 21, 2013. https://csc.asu.edu/2013/03/21/the-difference-between-story-and-narrative/.
Costa, Tom. "The Geography of Slavery in Virginia." Accessed September 9, 2023. http://www2.vcdh.virginia.edu/gos/.
Crookall, David, and Warren Thorngate, eds. "Acting, Knowing, Learning, Simulating, Gaming." Simulation and Gaming 40, no. 1 (2009): 8–26.
Daniels, Tim. "Photography Trends and Statistics (2023)." Lapse of the Shutter. June 13, 2023. https://www.lapseoftheshutter.com/photography-statistics/.
Darling, Linda Farr. "Using Artifacts to Foster Historical Inquiry." In *The Anthology of Social Studies: Issues and Strategies for Elementary Teachers*, edited by Roland Case and Penney Clark, 283–89. Vancouver, BC: Pacific Educational Press, 2008.
Darrow, Charles, and Elizabeth J. Magie. Monopoly. Pawtucket, RI: Hasbro, 1935. Board game.

Davidson, Liz. *Beyond Solitaire* (podcast audio). Accessed June 30, 2023. https://beyondsolitaire.buzzsprout.com/.

Davis, Barbara Gross. "Case Studies." In *Tools for Teaching*, 2nd ed., 222–29. San Francisco: Jossey-Bass, 2009.

Davis, Karyl A., M. Leslie Wade Zorwick, James Roland, and Melissa Maxcy Wade, eds. *Using Debate in the Classroom: Encouraging Critical Thinking, Communication, and Collaboration*. New York: Routledge, 2016.

Desai, Dipti, Jessica Hamlin, and Rachel Mattson. *History as Image, Image as History: Contemporary Art and Social Studies Education*. New York: Routledge, 2009.

Deslauriers, Louis, Logan S. McCarty, Kelly Miller, Kristina Callaghan, and Greg Kestin. "Measuring Actual Learning versus Feeling of Learning in Response to Being Actively Engaged in the Classroom." *Proceedings of the National Academy of Sciences* 116, no. 39 (September 2019): 19251–57.

Dixson, Dante D., and Frank C. Worrell. "Formative and Summative Assessment in the Classroom." *Theory Into Practice* 55, no. 2 (Spring 2016): 153–59.

Doyle, Terry. *Learner-Centered Teaching: Putting the Research on Learning into Practice*. New York: Routledge, 2011.

Eng, Dave. "Debriefing Games-Based Learning." *UniversityXP* (blog). February 1, 2022. https://www.universityxp.com/blog/2022/2/1/debriefing-games-based-learning.

———. *Experience Points* (podcast audio). https://www.universityxp.com/podcast.

Eaton, Dave. "Taking Cover: Explaining the Persistence of the Coverage Model in World History Surveys." *World History Connected*, February 2016. Accessed March 21, 2023. https://worldhistoryconnected.press.uillinois.edu/13.1/eaton.html.

Facing History and Ourselves. Accessed June 13, 2023. https://www.facinghistory.org/.

Felten, Peter. "Visual Literacy." *Change: The Magazine of Higher Learning* 40, no. 6 (2008): 60–64.

Flaherty, Colleen. "Scaling Up High-Impact Instruction." *Inside Higher Ed*, September 28, 2016. https://www.insidehighered.com/news/2016/09/28/new-grants-help-institutions-embed-reacting-past-other-high-impact-teaching.

Freeman, Mark. "Narrative as a Mode of Understanding: Method, Theory, Praxis." In *The Handbook of Narrative Analysis*, edited by Anna De Fina and Alexandra Georgakopoulou, 21–38. West Sussex, UK: John Wiley & Sons, 2015.

Frost, Jennifer. "Using 'Master Narratives' to Teach History: The Case of the Civil Rights Movement." *The History Teacher* 45, no. 3 (2012): 437–46.

Galarneau, Lisa. "Authentic Learning Experiences through Play: Games, Simulations and the Construction of Knowledge." *Proceedings of DiGRA 2005 Conference: Changing Views—Worlds in Play*. Vol. 3. Digital Games Research Association, 2005. http://www.digra.org/wp-content/uploads/digital-library/06276.47486.pdf.

Gaudelli, William. "Interpreting Democratic Images: Secondary Students' Reading of Visual Texts." *Teacher Education Quarterly* 36, no. 1 (2009): 111–30.

George, Elizabeth. "Life Lessons: A Game Takes Students to Renaissance Rome." *Perspectives on History: The Newsmagazine of the American Historical Association*, December 1, 2017.

Gerwin, David, and Jack Zevin. *Teaching U.S. History as Mystery*. 2nd ed. New York: Routledge, 2011.

Gooblar, David. *The Missing Course: Everything They Never Taught You about College Teaching*. Cambridge, MA: Harvard University Press, 2019.

Google Arts & Culture. Accessed June 23, 2023. https://artsandculture.google.com/.

Google Earth. "Education." Accessed June 29, 2003. https://www.google.com/earth/education/.

Grantham, Ashley, Emily Erin Robinson, and Diane Chapman. "'That Truly Meant a Lot to Me': A Qualitative Examination of Meaningful Faculty-Student Interactions." *College Teaching* 63, no. 3 (July 2015): 125–32.

"Guiding Principles for Choices Content Development." Choices Program Brown University. Accessed June 13, 2023. https://www.choices.edu/about/guiding-principles/.

Gurung, Regan A. R., Nancy L. Chick, Aeron Haynie, eds. *Signature Pedagogies: Approaches to Teaching Disciplinary Habits of Mind*. Sterling, VA: Stylus Publishing, 2009.

Hake, Clare, and Terry Haydn. "Stories or Sources?" *Teaching History*, no. 78 (1995): 20–22.

Hamel, Debra. *Trying Neaira: The True Story of a Courtesan's Scandalous Life in Ancient Greece*. New Haven: Yale University Press, 2003.

Hays, Lauren, and Mark Hayse. "Game On! Experiential Learning with Tabletop Games." In *The Experiential Library: Transforming Academic and Research Libraries through the Power of Experiential Learning*, edited by Pete McDonnell, 103–15. New York: Chandos, 2017.

Hayse, Mark. "Tabletop Games and 21st Century Skill Practice in the Undergraduate Classroom." *Teaching Theology & Religion* 21, no. 4 (2018): 288–302.

Heim, Ashley, and Emily Holt. "From Bored Games to Board Games: Student-Driven Game Design in the Virtual Classroom." *Journal of Microbiology & Biology Education* 22, no.1 (2021).

Herman, Mark. Churchill. Hanford, CA: GMT Games, 2015. Board game.

Hill, Jennifer. "Inventory of Aiko Herzig Yoshinaga Papers." Online Archive of California. October 31, 2019. https://oac.cdlib.org/findaid/ark:/13030/c8kp888m/entire_text/.

Howard, Jay. "How to Hold a Better Class Discussion." *The Chronicle of Higher Education*, May 23, 2019. https://www.chronicle.com/article/how-to-hold-a-better-class-discussion/.

Jaffee, David. "Thinking Visually as Historians: Incorporating Visual Methods." In Michael Coventry, Peter Felten, David Jaffee, Cecilia O'Leary, Tracey Weis, and Susannah McGowan, "Ways of Seeing: Evidence and Learning in the History Classroom." *Journal of American History* 92, no. 4 (2006): 1371–402.

Jamestown Rediscovery. "Explore the Artifacts." Accessed September 9, 2023. https://historicjamestowne.org/collections/artifacts/.

Jamison, Leslie. "The Enduring Allure of Choose Your Own Adventure Books." *The New Yorker*, September 12, 2022.

Jancer, Matt. "How You Wound Up Playing 'The Oregon Trail' in Computer Class." *Smithsonian Magazine*, July 22, 2016. https://www.smithsonianmag.com/innovation/how-you-wound-playing-em-oregon-trailem-computer-class-180959851/.

Jennings, Steven. "Questions to Facilitate the Use of Maps as Primary Sources in the Classroom." *The Social Studies* 104, no. 5 (2013): 201–6.

Jerrim, John, and Sam Sims. "When Is High Workload Bad for Teacher Wellbeing? Accounting for the Non-Linear Contribution of Specific Teaching Tasks." *Teaching & Teacher Education* 105 (September 2021). https://doi.org/10.1016/j.tate.2021.103395.

Johnson, David W., and Roger T. Johnson. "An Overview of Cooperative Learning." Cooperative Learning Institute. Accessed September 7, 2022. http://www.co-operation.org/what-is-cooperative-learning.

Jordanova, Ludmilla. *The Look of the Past: Visual and Material Evidence in Historical Practice*. Cambridge: Cambridge University Press, 2012.

Junior Normal Class of Fisk University, Nashville, Tennessee, Seated on Steps Outside of Building. N.D. [between 1890 and 1906]. Photograph. Nashville, TN. Library of Congress Prints and Photographs Division. https://www.loc.gov/item/94513859/.

Kapell, Matthew, and Andrew Elliott, eds. *Playing with the Past: Digital Games and the Simulation of History*. New York: Bloomsbury Academic, 2013.

Kemble, Fanny. *Journal of a Residence on a Georgia Plantation in 1838–1839*. Athens: University of Georgia Press, 1984.

Kennedy, Ruth. "In-Class Debates: Fertile Ground for Active Learning and the Cultivation of Critical Thinking and Oral Communication Skills." *International Journal of Teaching and Learning in Higher Education* 19, no. 2 (2007): 183–90.

Ketelle, Diane. "Introduction to the Special Issue: What Is Storytelling in the Higher Education Classroom?" *Storytelling, Self, Society* 13, no. 2 (2017): 143–50.

Kuh, George D. "High-Impact Educational Practices: What They Are, Who Has Access to Them, and Why They Matter." Washington DC: American Association of Colleges and Universities, 2008. Accessed July 12, 2023. https://provost.tufts.edu/celt/files/High-Impact-Ed-Practices1.pdf.

Kurlansky, Mark. *Salt: A World History*. New York: Penguin Books, 2003.

LaCombe, Michael. "Teaching with Games Roundtable Q&A—Michael LaCombe with the Authors." University of Pennsylvania. *Early American Studies Miscellany*, July 15, 2022. https://web.sas.upenn.edu/earlyamericanstudies/2022/07/15/teaching-with-games-roundtable-qa/.

Lane, Lisa M. "Constructing the Past Online: Discussion Board as History Lab." *The History Teacher* 47, no. 2 (February 2014): 197–207.

Lang, James M. *Distracted: Why Students Can't Focus and What You Can Do about It*. New York: Basic Books, 2020.

———. "How to Teach a Good First Day of Class." *The Chronicle of Higher Education*. Accessed July 22, 2023. https://www.chronicle.com/article/how-to-teach-a-good-first-day-of-class/.

———. "Stop Blaming Students for Your Listless Classroom." *The Chronicle of Higher Education*. September 29, 2014. https://www.chronicle.com/article/stop-blaming-students-for-your-listless-classroom/.

Lantis, Jeffrey S. "Ethics and Foreign Policy: Structured Debates for the International Studies Classroom." *International Studies Perspectives* 5, no. 2 (2004): 117–33.

Leff, Benjamin J. J. "Popular Culture as Historical Text: Using Mass Media to Teach American History." *The History Teacher* 50, no. 2 (2017): 227–54.

Leffler, Warren K. *Civil Rights March on Washington, D.C.* 1963. Photograph. Washington, DC. Library of Congress Prints and Photographs Division. https://lccn.loc.gov/2003654393.

Lemov, Doug. "A Vast Army of Terracotta Warriors: Just How Do We Teach History?" *Teach Like a Champion* (blog). January 16, 2014. https://teachlikeachampion.org/blog/vast-army-terracotta-warriors-just-teach-history/.

Leonhard, Christian, and Jason Matthews. "Founding Fathers: Planner's Guide to the Constitutional Convention." Sigel, IL: Jolly Roger Games, 2010.

———. Campaign Manager: 2008. Roseville, MN: Z-Man Games, 2009. Board game.

Library of Congress. "Dorothea Lange's 'Migrant Mother' Photographs in the Farm Security Administration Collection." Accessed June 20, 2023. https://guides.loc.gov/migrant-mother/images.

Library of Congress and Nebraska State Historical Society. "About the Letters from the Uriah W. Oblinger Collection." Prairie Settlement: Nebraska Photographs and Family Letters. Accessed May 17, 2023. https://memory.loc.gov/ammem/award98/nbhihtml/aboutoblinger.html.

Livingstone, M. Rebecca, Kelly McFall, and Abigail Perkiss. *Monuments and Memory-Making: The Debate over the Vietnam Veterans Memorial, 1981–1982*. Chapel Hill: University of North Carolina Press, 2023.

Lowey-Ball, ShawnaKim. "History by Text and Thing." *Perspectives on History*, February 26, 2020. https://www.historians.org/publications-and-directories/perspectives-on-history/march-2020/history-by-text-and-thing.

Madison, James H. "Teaching with Images." *OAH Magazine of History* 18, no. 2 (2004): 65–68.

Major, Claire Howell, Michael S. Harris, and Todd Zakrajsek. *Teaching for Learning: 101 Intentionally Designed Educational Activities to Put Students on the Path to Success.* New York: Routledge, 2016.

Maranges, Tommy, and Max Temkin. Secret Hitler (board game). Chicago: Goat Wolf & Cabbage, 2016.

Mayer, Brian. Freedom: The Underground Railroad. Freemont, OH: Academy Games, 2023. Board game.

Mayer, Brian, and Christopher Harris. *Libraries Got Game: Aligned Learning through Modern Board Games.* Chicago: ALA Editions, 2010.

McCall, Jeremiah. "Bibliography." Gaming the Past. Accessed June 28, 2023. https://gamingthepast.net/theory-practice/bibliography/.

———. "The Historical Problem Space Framework: Games as a Historical Medium." *Game Studies* 20, no. 3 (September 2020). http://gamestudies.org/2003/articles/mccall.

———. "Navigating the Problem Space: The Medium of Simulation Games in the Teaching of History." *The History Teacher* 46, no. 1 (November 2012): 9–28.

McKee, Gabriel, and Daniela Wolfin. "Re-Rolling the Past: Representations and Reinterpretations of Antiquity in Analog and Digital Games: Introduction." *ISAW Papers* 22 (July 21, 2022). https://archive.nyu.edu/bitstream/2451/63888/3/Re-Rolling%20the%20Past%20PDF.pdf.

McNett, Gabriel. "Using Stories to Facilitate Learning." *College Teaching* 64, no.4 (2016): 184–93. https://www.tandfonline.com/doi/full/10.1080/87567555.2016.1189389.

Meyers, Steven A. "Do Your Students Care Whether You Care about Them?" *College Teaching* 57, no. 4 (Fall 2009): 205–10.

Miller, Amy Chasteen, and Brooklyn Mills. "'If They Don't Care, I Don't Care': Millennial and Generation Z Students and the Impact of Faculty Caring." *Journal of the Scholarship of Teaching and Learning* 19, no. 4 (October 2019): 78–89.

Montgomery, R. A. *Journey Under the Sea*. 1978; reprint. Waitsfield: Chooseco, 2005.

Moreau, Daniel, and Jonathan Smith. "Teachers Helping Their Students Think Historically . . . at Last?" *The History Teacher* 54, no. 4 (August 2021): 731–57.

National Archives. "Mapping History." Accessed June 29, 2023. https://www.docsteach.org/tools/mapping-history.

Newfield, Denise. "From Visual Literacy to Critical Visual Literacy: An Analysis of Educational Materials." *English Teaching: Practice and Critique* 10, no. 1 (2011): 81–94.

Newman, Mark, and Jack Zevin. *Geography as Inquiry: Teaching About and Exploring the Earth as Our Home*. Lanham, MD: Rowman & Littlefield, 2016.

Nicholson, Scott. "Completing the Experience: Debriefing in Experiential and Educational Games." *Journal on Systemics, Cybernetics and Informatics* 11 (2012): 117–21.

Nix, Jearl, and C. H. Bohan. "Looking at the Past for Help in the Present: The Role of Historical Photos in Middle and Secondary History Classes." *Ohio Social Studies Review* 51, no. 2 (2014): 13–22.

Offutt, Bill. *The Fate of John Brown, 1859*. Reacting Consortium. Accessed July 12, 2023. https://reactingconsortium.org/games/johnbrown1859.

Ohman, August R. *Missionary Map of the World Showing Prevailing Religions of Its Various Nations and the Central Stations of All Protestant Missionary Societies*. N.D. [1902?]. Map. New York. Library of Congress Geography and Map Division. https://www.loc.gov/item/2017586281/.

Olwell, Russell, and Azibo Stevens. "'I Had to Double Check My Thoughts': How the Reacting to the Past Methodology Impacts First-Year College Student Engagement, Retention, and Historical Thinking." *The History Teacher* 48, no. 3 (May 2015): 561–72.

Oral History Association. Accessed July 3, 2013. https://oralhistory.org/.

Ormond, Barbara. "Enabling Students to Read Historical Images: The Value of the Three-Level Guide for Historical Inquiry." *The History Teacher* 44, no. 2 (2011): 179–90.

Parellada, Cristian, and Mario Carretero. "Digital Historical Maps in Classrooms. Challenges in History Education." In *History Education in the Digital Age*, edited by Mario Carretero, María Cantabrana, Cristian Parellada, 139–61. Cham, Switzerland: Springer 2022.

Payne, Phillip. "Skill Building through Game Building in a Public History Class." *Process: A Blog for American History*, May 12, 2016. http://www.processhistory.org/game-building/.

Pegler-Gordon, Anna. "Seeing Images in History." *Perspectives on History: The Newsmagazine of the American Historical Association*, February 1, 2006. https://www.historians.org/research-and-publications/perspectives-on-history/february-2006/seeing-images-in-history.

Percell, Jay C. "Lessons from Alternative Grading: Essential Qualities of Teacher Feedback." *Clearing House* 90, no. 4 (2017): 111–15.

Perello, Chris. The American Civil War. Bakersfield, CA: Decision Games, 2018. Board game.

Plass, Jan L., Bruce D. Homer, and Charles K. Kinzer. "Foundations of Game-Based Learning." Educational Psychologist 50, no. 4 (2015): 258–83.

Plass, Jan L., Richard E. Mayer, and Bruce D. Homer, eds. *Handbook of Game-Based Learning*. Cambridge, MA: MIT Press, 2020.

Proctor, Nicholas W. *Forest Diplomacy: Cultures in Conflict on the Pennsylvania Frontier, 1757*. Chapel Hill: University of North Carolina Press, 2022.

———. "Making History: The Breakup Microgame." Reacting Consortium. Accessed June 21, 2023. https://reactingconsortium.org/games/makinghistory.

———. *Reacting to the Past Game Designer's Handbook*, 4th ed. CreateSpace Independent Publishing Platform, 2018.

Prockter, J. *A Correct Map of the World Drawn from the Best Discoveries*. 1760? Map. [London?: Publisher not identified]. Library of Congress Geography and Map Division. https://www.loc.gov/item/2017585774/.

Puurtinen, Marjaana, Markus Nivala, and Arja Virta. "Visual Sources and Historical Thinking in Higher Education." *Nordidactica: Journal of Humanities and Social Science Education* 2015, no. 4 (2015): 1–20.

Rael, Patrick. "Bibliography of Work on Game Studies and History," *Ludica* (blog), October 3, 2021. https://boardgamegeek.com/blogpost/123281/bibliography-work-game-studies-and-history.

———. "Playing with the Past: Teaching Slavery with Board Games." *Perspectives on History: The Newsmagazine of the American Historical Association*, October 13, 2021. https://www.historians.org/research-and-publications/perspectives-on-history/november-2021/playing-with-the-past-teaching-slavery-with-board-games.

———. "Proposal for a History Course Built around Tabletop Games." *Ludica* (blog). April 2, 2017. https://boardgamegeek.com/blogpost/64059/proposal-history-course-built-around-tabletop-game.

Rajkovic, Aleksandra Ilic, Mirjana Senic Ruzic, and Bojan Ljujic. "Board Games as Educational Media: Creating and Playing Board Games for Acquiring Knowledge of History." *IARTEM* e-journal 11, no. 2 (2019).

Reacting Consortium. Accessed July 12, 2023. https://reactingconsortium.org.
Reacting Consortium. Reacting Faculty Lounge. Facebook group page (private). Accessed July 12, 2023. https://www.facebook.com/groups/reactingfacultylounge.
Reacting Consortium. "What Is Reacting." Accessed October 18, 2022. https://reactingconsortium.org/WIR-basics
Reaktion Books. "Animal Series." Accessed July 4, 2023. https://reaktionbooks.co.uk/series/animal.
Reinhartz, Judy, and Dennis Reinhartz. "'How Wide the World:' Geography, Maps, and the Teaching of American History." *OAH Magazine of History* 7, no. 3 (1993): 21–26.
Robbins, Bruce. "Commodity Histories." *PMLA* 120, no. 2 (2005): 454–63.
Robbins, Margaret. "Female Representation in Comics and Graphic Novels: Exploring Classroom Study with Critical Visual Literacy." *SIGNAL Journal* 38, no. 1 (2014): 11–15.
Rodwell, Grant. *Whose History? Engaging History Students through Historical Fiction.* Adelaide: University of Adelaide Press, 2013.
Rotberg, Robert I. "Biography and Historiography: Mutual Evidentiary and Interdisciplinary Considerations." *The Journal of Interdisciplinary History* 40, no. 3 (2010): 305–24.
Sartwell, Crispin. *End of Story: Toward an Annihilation of Language and History.* Albany: State University of New York Press, 2000.
Schieble, Melissa. "Reading Images in 'American Born Chinese' through Critical Visual Literacy." *The English Journal* 103, no. 5 (2014): 47–52.
Schocker, Jessica B. "A Case for Using Images to Teach Women's History." *The History Teacher* 47, no. 3 (2014): 421–50.
Schrier, Karen. *Learning, Education & Games*, 3 vols. Pittsburgh: Carnegie Mellon University, 2014–19.
Shoemaker, Nancy L. "Where Is the History Lab Course?" *Perspectives on History*, January 1, 2009. https://www.historians.org/publications-and-directories/perspectives-on-history/january-2009/where-is-the-history-lab-course.
Silver, Naomi. "Reflective Pedagogies and the Metacognitive Turn in College Teaching." In *Using Reflection and Metacognition to Improve Student Learning: Across the Disciplines, Across the Academy*, edited by Matthew Kaplan, Naomi Silver, Danielle LaVaque-Manty, and Deborah Meizlish, pp. 1–17. Sterling, VA: Stylus Publishing, 2013.
Sipress, Joel M., and David J. Voelker. "The End of the History Survey Course: The Rise and Fall of the Coverage Model." *The Journal of American History* 97, no. 4 (2011): 1050–66. https://www.jstor.org/stable/41508915.
———. "From Learning History to Doing History: Beyond the Coverage Model." In *Exploring Signature Pedagogies: Approaches to Teaching Disciplinary Habits of Mind*, edited by Regan A. R. Gurung, Nancy L. Chick, and Aeron Haynie, 19–35. Sterling, VA: Stylus Publishing, 2009.
SlaveVoyages Consortium. Accessed September 22, 2022. https://www.SlaveVoyages.org.

Smithsonian Institution. National Museum of the American Indian. Accessed July 3, 2023. https://americanindian.si.edu/.
Smithsonian Institution. National Postal Museum. Accessed July 3, 2023. https://postalmuseum.si.edu/.
Smithsonian Institution. Smithsonian Learning Lab. Accessed June 23, 2023. https://learninglab.si.edu/.
Society for History Education, Inc. "*The History Teacher*: Gaming in the History Classroom." Accessed June 28, 2023. https://www.societyforhistoryeducation.org/games.html.
Srole, Carole, Christopher Endy, and Birte Pfleger. "Active Learning in History Survey Courses: The Value of 'In-Class' Peer Mentoring." *The History Teacher* 51, no. 1 (2017): 89–102.
Suh, Yonghee. "Past Looking: Using Arts as Historical Evidence in Teaching History." *Social Studies Research and Practice* 8, no. 1 (2013): 135–59.
Sweet, Julie Anne. "Making History Come Alive: The Boston Massacre Trials." *The History Teacher* 54, no. 3 (May 2021): 509–38.
Tally, Bill, and Lauren B. Goldenberg. "Fostering Historical Thinking with Digitized Primary Sources." *Journal of Research on Technology in Education* 38, no. 1 (2005): 1–21.
Townsend, Robert B. "Has the Decline in History Majors Hit Bottom?" *Perspectives on History: The Newsmagazine of the American Historical Association*, February 23, 2021. https://www.historians.org/research-and-publications/perspectives-on-history/march-2021/has-the-decline-in-history-majors-hit-bottom-data-from-2018%E2%80%9319-show-lowest-number-since-1980.
Vanzant, Kevin. "Problems with Narrative in the U.S. Survey and How Fiction Can Help." *The History Teacher* 52, no. 4 (2019): 677–96.
Vecchiola, Carla. "Digging in the Digital Archives: Engaging Students in an Online American History Survey." *The History Teacher* 53, no. 1 (2019): 107–34.
Volk, Steven S. "How to Navigate an 'Upside-Down' World: Using Images in the History Classroom." *New Directions for Teaching & Learning* 2015, no. 141 (Spring 2015): 53–65.
von der Beck, Ina, Ulrike Cress, and Aileen Oeberst. "Is There Hindsight Bias without Real Hindsight? Conjectures Are Sufficient to Elicit Hindsight Bias." *Journal of Experimental Psychology: Applied* 25, no. 1 (August 2018): 88–99. https://doi.org/10.1037/xap0000185.
Walker, Susannah, and Gustavo Carrera. "Developing a Signature Pedagogy for the High School U.S. History Survey: A Case Study." *The History Teacher* 51, no. 1 (2017): 65–88.
Ware, Susan. "Writing Women's Lives: One Historian's Perspective." *The Journal of Interdisciplinary History* 40, no. 3 (2010): 413–35.
Watson, C. Edward, and Thomas Chase Hagood, eds. *Playing to Learn with Reacting to the Past: Research on High Impact, Active Learning Practices*. Cham, Switzerland: Palgrave Macmillan, 2018.
Werner, Walter. "Reading Visual Texts." *Theory and Research in Social Education* 30, no. 2 (2002): 401–28.

Wiley, Jennifer, and Ivan K. Ash. "Multimedia Learning of History." In *The Cambridge Handbook of Multimedia Learning*, edited by Richard E. Mayer, 375–92. Cambridge: Cambridge University Press, 2005. https://doi.org/10.1017/CBO9780511816819.025.

Wills, Jr., John E. "Lives and Other Stories: Neglected Aspects of the Teacher's Art." *The History Teacher* 26, no. 1 (1992): 33–49. https://doi.org/10.2307/494084.

Wineburg, Sam. *Historical Thinking and Other Unnatural Acts: Charting the Future of Teaching the Past*. Philadelphia: Temple University Press, 2001.

———. "Thinking Like a Historian." *Teaching with Primary Sources Quarterly* 3, no. 1 (Winter 2010): 2–4.

Worthington, Tracy Anne. "Letting Students Control Their Own Learning: Using Games, Role-Plays, and Simulations in Middle School U.S. History Classrooms." *Social Studies* 109 no. 2 (May 2018): 136–50.

Zare, Pezhman, and Moomala Othman. "Classroom Debate as a Systematic Teaching/Learning Approach." *World Applied Sciences Journal* 28, no. 11 (2013): 1506–13.

———. "Students' Perceptions toward Using Classroom Debate to Develop Critical Thinking and Oral Communication Ability." *Asian Social Science* 11, no. 9 (2015): 158–70.

Zevin, Jack, and David Gerwin. *Teaching World History as Mystery*. New York: Routledge, 2011.

About the Author

Elizabeth George is associate professor of history at Taylor University in Upland, Indiana, and oversees the Social Studies Education major. She writes and speaks about games and learning and other innovative pedagogies.

Milton Keynes UK
Ingram Content Group UK Ltd.
UKHW011640100524
442543UK00015B/150